Publish by:
Afrocentric Schools Nig. Ltd.

© Ubong Alfred 2016

This book cannot be reproduce by any means; Graphic, electronic or mechanical, including photocopying, recording, taping or by any information storage and retrieval system without the written permission of the copy right holder except in the case of brief quotation embodied in critical articles and review.

All bible quotation is taken from THE GIDEONS INTERNATIONAL VERSION.

ISBN: 978-978-54456-0-2

Afrocentric Schools Nig. Ltd.
No. 105 Rumuagholu road (off Rumuokoro roundabout)
Obio Akpor LGA, Rivers state.
Email; afrocentricschool@gmail.com
Website; www.afrocentricgroup.com
Phone; 08189151137. 08068353548

Marketed by AFROCENTRIC and her affiliate
Port Harcourt
    Aguma's Bookshop Nigeria, beside First Bank, Uniport, Port Harcourt. 08066055992.
    Garrison Bus-stop Book Stand.
Uyo
    Worldwork Bookshop, 67 Oron Road, Akwa-Ibom State
    felix@worldbookshop.com. 08021495858, 08037091479

Dedication

This book is dedicated to all those who quest for Knowledge, and those who were killed for the liberation of the black man mind, the true men of God.

Introduction

The greatest fraud in human history is currently unveiling itself; men ascribe the title 'man of God' to themselves and on the process milk the populace, convincing them in the name of God and promises of blessing and upliftment. Men are currently covertly exploiting the masses in the name of God.

These men portray themselves as evidence of God's blessing while in reality, their congregation is the source of their blessings. The greatest fraud in human history is when man assign his success to another man who he thought and believed helped him spiritually to achieved his physical need. The greatest fraud in human history is when men substitute lie for truth and truth for lie. It is when men depend virtually on others for a living rather than themselves.

The greatest fraud in human history is what we unveil in this book.

Men of God, are they actually real? Do you know if actually you are constantly brainwashed by these 'men of God' and the society at large? Do you know how much you are indoctrinated which facilitate you falling prey to these acclaimed men of God?

But what/who is God? Are some humans truly God representatives? Is religion the only institution that hold the answer to the question of who/what is God? Could it not be found in science, engineering, psychology, politics, technology etc?

Before the present religions came into existence, people always believed in God, a supernatural being. The ancient Africans, Greek and the Romans worship different Gods at various times and mankind has always strived to discover the true God, the force of nature, the laws and form of existence. Christianity, Islam, Hindus, Technology, spiritualism, science, Judaism, philosophy, Meta physics etc. all evolved in the quest for an answer to one ultimate question; what/who is God?

Currently, the leaders of the Christian movement ascribe to themselves God's representatives, God's personal assistance and God's right hand men; they ascribe the titled, 'man of God' to themselves and claim to be his representative here on earth and in the process defrauding and misleading millions of people to mental slavery.

This book point out those throughout history who truly access God, who in the real sense and definition of God, truly are his semblance, the true men of God.

Cognitive dissonance which I define as the natural resistant of truth after years of believing in lies, may prevent many from absorbing the reality and self-revealing truth presented in this book, yet in their inner conscience, it will be there.

It is in Christianity that men claim to be God's representative; it is in Christianity that men ascribe to themselves the title of 'man of God'. It is in Christianity that the greatest and biggest fraud in human history is currently unveiling. Islam is unveiling the biggest resistant movement in the world.

I subscribe to the truth, which is God is nature and no religion knows or perhaps tell the truth. A religion that portrays itself as God's institution is fraud.

Religion is an ideology, a political-social movement. It has always been so right from the time of the Roman Empire; it is a big business and control mechanism for the elite. The average man portrays religion as God's institution, for the political class it is a control mechanism and political movement. It is at this vantage point we adopt Christianity in portraying a true man of God.

The answer to the ultimate question, who is God, can only be found if you, stop child religious indoctrination. A legislation that prohibit parent from forcing their children to participate in religious activities and programs, then a self-reviling truth will emancipate and a wild fire of freedom will be unleashed in Africa.

The tone of this book gradually shifts from the norm to the reality, from religion to reality, from superstition to reality.

Chapter one compares the present day Christian religious leaders with the attribute of the Christian God and came out with a perfect description of a true man of God. A man of God is different from a religious leader and most of the present day men of God are actually religious leaders and in business sense, they are con artist.

The entire system and doctrine of Pentecostal movement is packaged to generate money for the owners of the churches, they constantly brainwash their members to believe and act in certain direction while their lifestyle portray the opposite, these inconsistencies is what I elaborate to open the reasoning faculty of the populace.

At the end, you will discover that most of the acclaimed men of God are actually business men offering consultancy services and hope.

Yes, churches offer the services of given hope to people and take their fee through tithe, offering and other form of donation.

Chapter two progresses to answer the question who a true man of God is, using the bible and comparison with men who were called men of God in the bible. I discovered that Moses, David and the rest were called men of God and they were not preachers or religious leaders.

I went back to history to showcase men who were truly of God. These are men who share the attribute of God and that of those which the bible addresses as men of God. They are true men of God in Africa.

This eye opener shows that a man of God must not always be a religious leader but can be a political, educational or even a revolutionary leader. As a matter of fact, men of God are always true liberators, people who fought to liberate their people from oppression and slavery.

I repeat some quotations, this is to enable the reader ascertain the true meaning of a true man of God.

Chapter three spelled out what actually is true sin and what is good, all in consonant with the Bible and the lifestyle of the true men of God. For years, religion has convinced people to believe in absurdities as the truth and the truth as absurd.

We spell out base on Bible principle what actually constitute a sin. We discovered that the action itself is not a sin but the purpose of the action. Free yourself from mental slavery, think and follow the ways of the biblical men of God.

Chapter four gives various views and definition of God by various religions and persons and concluded that God is nature; the trees, the animals, human, mountains, the sun etc. The entire universe embodied the laws of nature, the entire universe embodied God. Science is the study of God; technology is the only true miracle.

Chapter five is revelation, it showcase how best to access God personally without passing through these so called men of God who mostly are wolf in sheep clothing. Our present men of God are mostly con men, business men and religious entertainers.

Here I reveal the most hidden secret of the universe, the magnetic nature of the human mind, I reveal the strategies and principles adopted by these so called men of God to con the general populace. Faith and your state of mind is the center of the human energy and it can be activated mostly externally to produce "miracle"

Truth is the truth; it is undisputable and can be prove beyond reasonable doubt. A generally acceptable idea is not an evident of truth. After all, the entire world once believes that the earth is flat; does the general acceptability of this theory make it the truth? of course No!

What is presented here deserve your attention. Think of it, give it a try, it will dawn on you that you have been under deceit for years.

Open your mind to this truth, do not allow cognitive dissonance to disenfranchise you from benefitting from this truth by liberating yourself from the clutches of these so called men of God who continuously and consistently brainwash you into giving to them, they consistently prophesy unrealistically and work on your mind to enslave you. Think.

Table of Content

Dedication	ii
Introduction	iii - vii
CHAPTER ONE Religious Leaders or Men of God	1
CHAPTER TWO True Men of God	36
CHAPTER THREE Good Versus Evil, The Reality	122
CHAPTER FOUR What/Who is God	138
CHAPTER FIVE How to Access God	158
Bibliography	177
Index	179

CHAPTER ONE

RELIGIOUS LEADERS OR MEN OF GOD?

Who will I tell what I have seen? How am I to explain all I have known? Africa is crumbling on our feet, men are enslaving others in the name of God.

These men, most of which undergo training from Bible school or apprenticeship, with their wives founded a church with an accompanied title of a pastor, prophet, evangelist, bishop or reverend; they all are called men of God by virtue of their position and religious leadership.

These men stand on the church pulpit every Sunday to pour 'the blessing of God' on you, to proclaim the love Jesus have for you, to prophesy good things for you, to heal your sickness and give you wealth, are they truly of God? Is your pastor truly a man of God?

"Someone is blessed today" shouted your pastor

"Amen" thundered the congregation. Is it truly of God?

In Christendom, religious leaders are equated to men of God. This misconception is the major source of confusion. Must a man of God be a religious leader? Can a non-religious leader be a man of God? Is religion the only institution of God? Is religion an institution of God? The Bible makes us understand that a man of God must not always be a religious preacher.

WHO IS A TRUE MAN OF GOD?

The best way to ascertain who a true man of God is; is to know who is God and to study the life of those who were given the title, men of God in the Bible. According to the Bible, God is an embodiment of many attribute. A true man of God shares some or the entire attributes of God and that of the biblical men of God.

What should a man of God be like?

From biblical view, the following people were at one point called men of God.

David; Nehemiah 12;24

> *"And the heads of the levites were Hashabiah, Sherebiah, and Joshua the son of Kadmiel, with their brothers across from them, to praise and gives thanks, group alternating with group, according to the command of David the man of God"*

Moses; Deuteronomy 33;1

> *"Now this is the blessing with which Moses the man of God blessed the children of Israel before his death"*

Elijah; 1 King 17;18 'So she said to Elijah,

> *"what have I to do with you, O man of God? Have you come to me to bring my sin to remembrance, and to kill my son?"*

Elisha; 2 King 4;1-7

> *"A certain woman of the wives of the sons of the prophets cried out to Elisha saying....Then she came and told the man of God. And he said, "Go, sell the oil and pay your debt; and you and your son live on the rest."*

Others; 1 Timothy 6:10-11

> *"For the love of money is a root of all kinds of evil, for which some have strayed from the faith in their greediness, and pierced themselves through with many sorrows. But you, O man of God, flee these things and pursue righteousness, godliness, faith, love, patience, gentleness.*

Others were figuratively addressed as servant of God or friends of God. In essence, they were equally God representative here on earth. These people are;
Abraham; Genesis 20;2-7

> 'Now Abraham said of Sarah his wife, "she is my sister" And Abimelech King of Gerar sent and took Sarah... Now therefore, restore the man's wife; for he is a prophet, and he will pray for you and you shall live. But if you do not restore her, know that you shall surely die, you and all who are yours.'"

James 2;23 'And the scripture was fulfilled which says,
> "Abraham believed God, and it was accounted to him as righteousness."
And he was called the friend of God.'

Isaiah; Isaiah 20;3,
> 'Then the LORD said, "Just as my servant Isaiah has walked naked and barefoot three years for a sign and a wonder against Egypt and Ethiopia'

MUST A MAN OF GOD BE A RELIGIOUS LEADER

David was never a prophet or pastor; he was a soldier and a king yet he was called man of God. Moses was not in the true sense of the word a prophet; he led a revolutionary movement to free the Israelite from Egypt yet he was called man of God.

Abraham was not a preacher, he owns no congregation yet he was a prophet and a friend of God which is even a greater title than man of God. Samuel was a political Godfather and a seer, he anointed the first two kings of Israel.

Why did the bible address these men as men of God?

They were all out to free their people and their generation. Moses freed the Israelites from Egypt, David conquered the philistines by killing goliath and conquered all his enemies, Abraham moved to a new land to establish a free and sovereign nation and introduced religion to the world. He did not accept the religion of his settler but established his own religion.

It is within this context that we see the perfect description of a man of God. He is one who acts as a shepherd to those "sheep" in his care not as a wolf devouring their money. A true man of God must not always be a religious leader. The man who will salvage Africa, our savior, our messiah will be a political ideology leader.

Political ideology I define as a concept of leadership with a single idea.

We believe in true independence; an economic, political, cultural, technological and religious self-reliance

We believe in freedom of organization, the current African countries must be resolved, and an all-African referendum will hold to give birth to new African nations

Those are political ideologies.

IS RELIGION THE ONLY INSTITUTION OF GOD

Absolutely NO, Before Abraham there was no Abrahamic religion; Judaism, Christianity and Islam, but there was God and Abraham was a friend of God even before religion was founded, that God was certainly not a religious God because they was no religion.

All the biblical men of God share a common characteristic; they were all liberators. For ages, liberators have been born into different region, peoples and professions. These men have changed the world without religious influence. Thomas Sankara change Burkina Faso within two years without prayer, fasting or any other religious dogma.

Religion is not the only institution of God. Recently, science and weaponry technology has been used to liberate people, and to destroy people even more than as God destroyed Sodom and Gomorrah. Science and technology is equally or even a greater institution of God because it truly liberate and uplift humanity. The pioneers of scientific and technological innovations are more of God than the religious leaders.

GODS ATTRIBUTE AND RELIGIOUS LEADERS

Attribute is defined as the character, attitude and quality of a person or group of people.

Here we compare the attribute of the biblical God and the biblical men of God, with that of the current acclaimed men of God and come up with a clear picture of whom or what a man of God should be like. Here are the attributes of God.

Providence

Providence simply means care.

Psalm 4;8

> *'I will both lie down in peace, and sleep; for you alone,*
> *O Lord, makes me dwell in safety'*

Philippians 4;19
> *'And my God shall supply all your need according to his*
> *riches in glory by Christ Jesus'*

Providence is difference from miracle, providence means real care while miracle is expected and supernatural care. If I'm drowned in a sea, I will expect God or a man of God to send me a rescue boat, this is care. The idea of miraculous rescue through disappearance or some shark or dolphin carry me to the shore is what many people expect today; miracle.

When Jesus referred to us as "sheep," He was not speaking in affectionate terms. In truth, sheep rank among the dumbest animals in creation. A stray sheep, still within earshot of the herd, becomes disoriented, confused, frightened, and incapable of finding its way back to the flock. Unable to ward off hungry predators, the stray is perhaps the most helpless of all creatures.

Entire herds of sheep are known to have drowned during times of flash flooding even in sight of easily accessible higher ground. Like it or not, when Jesus called us His sheep, He was saying that without a shepherd, we are helpless.

An entire race may be drown without a good shepherd, a true man of God

The shepherd is one who has several roles in regard to his sheep. He leads, feeds, nurtures, comforts, corrects and protects.

The question is: Is your pastor leading, feeding, nurturing, comforting, correcting and protecting you? He who feed the soul while ignoring the body will soon have a roaming soul without a body. The idea of spiritual food is an illusion of the highest order, feed the body and the soul will be fed. Church expects you to sow seed but they never sow a seed in your life and the community, instead they make you believe the reward will come from heaven. What is good for the goose is good for the baboon.

The dependent of Africa on other block of the world, the level of poverty in Africa, the underdevelopment of Africa, the high rate of mortality in Africa are all circumstantial evidence that Africa is a drowning sheep in need of a shepherd, it point to the fact, truth and reality that the current crops of pastors in Africa are not men of God, they are not Good shepherd, instead of nurturing you, you unconsciously nurture them, instead of leading you, they consistently mislead you, instead of feeding you, you are feeding them, instead of protecting you, you protect them, instead of enlightening and freeing the mind of the people, they are tirelessly working to enslave them.

They only offer hope and comfort, something naturally you can keep alive by yourself when you set your mind. Men build men and the society not God.

Moses was a man of God, he provided water by striking a rock, prays for manner and nurtured his people, and he divided the red sea to cross his people to safety. All these occur instantly according to the bible, He never demanded any jewelries or money from them, he never demanded for seed sowing. This was providence.

David was a man of God, he fought Goliath out of his will, he was not persuaded to do it but he did it for the love of his people.

Independence

The independence of God means God is so independent that he does not need us. It is based on Acts 17:24-25, where it says that "God, who made the world and everything in it, since he is Lord of heaven and earth, does not dwell in temples made with hands. Nor is He worshiped with men's hands, as though He needed anything, since He gives to all life, breath, and all things".

This is also referred to as the sovereignty of God. This is often related to God's self-existence and his self-sufficiency.

God does not need our worship nor dwell in the temple made of hand neither does he need anything from us. A true man of God lead people to self-sufficient and true independent; the understanding of the fact that we are embodiment of God, we are part of God, we do not need external God, we seek the God that is in us.

True men of God free the mind of the people from dependency. They proclaim economic independence, cultural independence, political independence and religious independence. Moses a man of God proclaimed the political independence of Israel when he stood with pharaoh and utters the word recorded on Exodus 5;1 "...Thus says the Lord God of Israel: 'Let my people go, that they may hold a feast to me in the wilderness.'"

Elijah proclaims religious independence when he challenges the prophet of Baal. Don't get this wrong, Elijah was fighting for the God of his forefathers because they are of his forefathers, his ancestors. Baal was a foreign God introduce just as Christianity and Islam were introduced in Africa. We abandon ours, and fight for a foreign God, Elijah hold on to his and fought against the domination of the foreign God. He challenged them on a contest of death, "The God who answered by fire, let him be our God", he said.

A true man of God must be so independent that he does not need the follower but only direct them to God. He must be a preacher of an ideology. If your church doesn't preach true developmental ideologies anchor on reasoning, reality and scientific methods, then he is not of God, he does not direct people to God but tend to hold them together in chain for his personal benefit.

Such pastor's interest is to depend on your tithe and offering, which satisfy his physical need while asking you to wait for your blessing, a spiritual need. Such preachers are mere religious leaders not men of God. A true man of God directs you to true independence, independent as a people, independent as God.

They makes you to believe that whatever success you've achieved in your life does not have anything to do with your hard work but with your relationship with God, while in reality your hard work and mental ability is your sustaining force. They did this to create dependency. God is independent why will a man of God create a dependency? You depend on him for miracle, and he depends on you for money and sustenance of the system.

If your church ever advertise miracle, your pastor is not of God. It is only the word of God that ought to be advertise, the liberation of the mind from political, economic, technological, cultural and religious bondage in Africa. That is the true word of God for Africa.

I have heard people attributing their success to the God of their pastor or church. This is pastor worshiping, a complete derail from Christianity concept.

This is a call for all present men of God to free the mind of the people, tell them that you don't need them. Tell them that they don't need you, that they have access to God. Tell them that the only way to financial success is good financial education, perseverance, imagination, knowledge and self-discipline. Tell them they need good medical attention when they are sick than they need your prayers. Tell them that whatever predicament they find themselves; they can fight back with knowledge not prayer, with planning not fasting, with motivated desire not divine intervention. Tell them that God does not dwell in temples made of hands nor need our worship according to Act 17;25. Tell them the true word of God.

Free the peoples mind, tell them the truth. Anything contrary to telling the truth about the independence of God which abides in us, is not of God since we are his embodiment.

Love

Exodus 6;6

"wherefore say to the children of Israel; I will bring you out from under the burdens of the Egyptians, and I will rescue you from their bondage, and I will redeem you with an outstretched arm, and with great judgment"

The God of the Old Testament display love to his choosing people, the Israelites. He inflicted pains on the Egyptians to force them let his people go. He took them out of oppression; this is the true love of God.

He assisted the Israelites in killing and maiming peoples who obstruct their way as they match to the promise land. He led them to many victories in war.

A true man of God must be an embodiment of true love to his people in all it ramification because God is love, he must be free of greed. He must free his people from bondage; from economic, political, social, cultural, technological and religious bondage.

When a pastor said "show love to God, give to him" it is a lie, you can only show love to your fellow human, your brother and honor God. Ask.

1) Does your pastor ever made a huge donation to a noble course outside the church and her related activities and personal businesses?

2) The schools establish by your pastors, do they give scholarship to indigent student?

3) The school, do they charge the highest fee or a fee that can accommodate the poorest family?

4) The excess money made by your pastor (I choose not to use church) what exactly do they used it for? Expansion of the

church empire and deceit, or research and technology which is the true study of God?
5) Does your man of God insist that you give to the poor instead of the church?
6) Does your man of God ever preach the message of emancipation and true independent?
7) Has your man of God ever oppose injustice in the land?
8) Has he ever build a road or provide light for the community his church is located?

When a company is located in our community, we expect them to provide community services but when a church who makes profit more than the company is sited in the same community, nobody ask for community services. If a company can show love, what stop God from showing love when he is an embodiment of love, unless of course it is a fake God in a fake church lead by a fake man of God.

You cannot call yourself a man of God while you cheat people or lie to them or fool them or control them to your own advantage. You cannot say you love God and twist His Word to your own advantage.

Your pastor never support a noble cause which he stand not to benefit, covertly or openly, this is the attitude of a business man not a true man of God. You cannot be an embodiment of love while charging the highest fee for school built from people's donations.

Love becomes the basis of the creation, the commandment, the gospel and the criterion for judgment. The recent happening in the church proves a love gap between the flock and the shepherd. Now, it is the sheep who nurture, feed, protect and comfort the shepherd. It is the masses(sheep) contributing to the church(shepherd) and the church never give back anything tangible, devoid of profit to the society rather than the expectation and fulfillment of magic, called miracle. It transforms the mental attitude of the people to be so dependent on magic, an ancient mythology and it entirely kills the collective creative ability of the people, thereby distorting our thinking processes, hindering the development of science and technology, the true study of God.

The current shepherds are mostly business men whose intention is to lead the sheep and milk them for profits.

Veracity

The veracity of God means he is truth personified. Titus 1:2 refers to "...God, who cannot lie." It means free from sin or guilt; sin of deceit, manipulation, It means that whatever you do must be the truth.

What is truth? Truth is anything which can be proven beyond reasonable doubt to be real or factual.

Is your pastor telling the truth just as Moses told the Jew that was beating his brother, "why beat up your brother"?

Is your pastor telling the truth just as David said, this goliath is nothing, I will fight and defeat him for the sake of my people.

Is your pastor telling the truth by returning the money he gets from the community through tithes and offering back to the community by providing affordable education, social amenities etc. or is he violating 1 timothy 6;10-11

Veracity can be detected through action and word.

1)   Has your pastor ever say that you are not contributing to the world without winning soul or without donating to the church? Could it not be that God also want Christians to

serve the world as doctors, scientists, builders etc.? A theology that elevates the soul while subtly devaluing the rest of the body is disastrous for the individual believer and the society as a whole.

2) Has your man of God ever say, whatever measures you give to God, so shall his blessing be to you? Do you think God will ignore you because you did not donate to the church? This is a lie, your blessing is hinged on your mental capacity and mind (spirit) otherwise called determinate motive driven purpose?

3) Does your man of God attach price to the service he renders to you? Do you pay to speak with your man of God? Do you pay directly or indirectly to receive blessing? Do you pay your pastor for consultancy services which ought to be offered by consultancy firm, in the guise of counseling?

4) Does your pastor sell holy water, holy handkerchief, holy sand and other holy things? When Jesus sends Holy Spirit to his disciples, he did not demand for any type of payment; praise, sacrifice or money etc.
The truth is that all these are lies and cheap manipulations.
If God is truth personified, if God cannot lie, then a true man of God must not lie. But today, we are witnesses to various forms of lies, deceit and manipulations in the church.

The so called counseling are always lies yet we keep on looking for new places. Don't be among the gullible, docile, stupid and brainless followers. Free yourself now.

Imagine the power Peter had over men when he raised the cripple? Act 3;1-8 Do you see him telling the people that they must pay him for blessing or to enable them do the same? Imagine what Paul could ask of those who witnessed when a deadly snake hung on him and nothing happened to him? Act 28; 3-5. Does the Bible not record him saying he wants no man's money but prefers to pay his own way himself? Read your bible. These were Christian leaders - they believed God's reward is in the next world.

Today, Tithing and seed sowing is now preached every day in the church. The fake men of God ask you to bring to them and wait for your reward in heaven. Why did they ask you to donate for a reward? Is it an investment? It is a pure case of hypnosis.

Why didn't they wait for their reward in heaven? Why can't they pray to God to bless the church without you? Why didn't they ask God to send the church reward from heaven?

Most pastors equally give but ultimately to themselves. They give scholarship in their schools, they share the harvest given by members to other members, and they donate a car they get through the church to the church. Wake up brothers and sisters and understand their intrigue.

They knew blessing does not come directly from God, so they turn you to their source of blessing and abandoned you to seek for yours, in which they make you believe it's equally made possible by them.

This is manipulation displayed technically, hypnosis, brainwash and deceit.
Why did they sell Holy Spirit? Did Christ or any of the prophets of old sell Holy Spirit? Elijah, after proving to all that his God is greater than Baal, he did not engage in the selling of holy fire like many prophets will do today.

Today they sell holy spirit inform of holy water, holy handkerchief, holy sand and holy pen. They sometimes sell holy magic by telling you to run to the pulpit and donate in other to received blessing or pay a certain amount to shake hand with the man of God.
I met a pastor who announced in church that his jeep is for sale; his intent is to donate the money to the church new building project. Where did he get the jeep from? Who owns the church? On the CAC registration certificate, who are the trustees; the same pastor. In essence he is donating to himself what he got from others. That's an act of manipulation; he should sell it and donates to orphanage, which is giving in the real sense.

The essence of setting up the organization (The Church), how does it put food directly on the teeming population of poor Africans? Ask, If we are saved through Christ, are we really saved? What exactly does it means for someone to be saved? What is the definition of a savior?
Africa is in dare need of a savior who will tell them the truth and liberate them from dependency and poverty because God does not tell lies. Churches today are built on the foundation of lies and

deceit while the God they claim to worship does not lie.

Omniscience

A true man of GOD must be all knowing. Deuteronomy 18:21-22, *"And if you say in your heart, How shall we know the word which the LORD has not spoken? When a prophet speaks in the name of the LORD, if the thing does not happen or come to pass, that is the thing which the LORD has not spoken; the prophet has spoken it presumptuously; you shall not be afraid of him."*

Does your man of God, pastor, reverend, bishop, prophet, evangelist, father, cardinal or arch bishop or .... Ever speak that which never comes to pass? Then he is not of God but a mere religious leader.

His relentless fulfill prophesies are mere coincident if only one, just one of his prophesy does not come to fulfillment.

In a gathering of people, there is always probability of someone who need a husband, who is sick in the stomach, who need job, who experience pain in one part of his body etc., your pastor pronouncement of these is not a prophesy, it does not make him omniscient.

Has your man of God ever pointed to a specific person, a specific event and said this is the specific thing that will happen and it comes to pass each and every time? Ask yourself and you shall realize if your pastor is a true man of God.

How many times did he does this, and how many times does he succeed? One failure, yes one failure indicates that he or she is not a true man of God.

The true Prophet of the Lord predicts that which does come to pass. If the Prophet's predictions fail, they are exposed as not of God.

Jeremiah 28:9,

> *"As for the prophet who prophesies of peace, when the word of the prophet comes to pass, the prophet will be known as one whom the LORD has truly sent."*

The prediction of a true man of God must be 100% accurate, No 'if' or 'or', it must be specific. Also note that some acclaimed men of God can predict with 100% accuracy but still they are not from God. You will identify this people when one of their predictions fails to come to pass.

It is crucial that we examine each prediction of the prophet to prove his omniscience, a single failure, and then understand in your heart that you are dealing with a dyed in the wool, psychologically sound false man of God.

In today's spiritual churches and Pentecostal movements, prophesies is the order of the day but if you are an ardent observer of these prophesies, you will discover the following;

1) They are general prophesies, it is not directed to a specific person. This is psychology, in a gathering of people, someone is expendable. They prey on probability. This is evident that the religious leader is not omniscience, hence he is not a true man of God.

2) The healings are mostly staged.
3) Individual prophesies are always doom, and then the man of God offer solution which involve money. This is done to create dependency.
4) General prophesy is also about blessing and good fortune helping to re-enforce the mind of the people to believe in magic called miracle above reality and keep them faithful and hoping.

If a single specific prophesy of your acclaimed man of God fail to come to fruition, know that you are led by a fake man of God, don't ignore such failure, don't create an alibi to cover it, just understand that he is a fake man of God, a religious leader.

Recently, some acclaimed men of God predicted that former president of Nigeria, president Jonathan will win re-election but he failed, that was the word which the Lord has not spoken.

Impeccability

Impeccability means the state of being perfect without fault, incapable of wrong doing. God is so natural, he is balance, he is perfection, he is natural laws, he is the universe.

James 1:13

> "Let no one say when he is tempted, "I am tempted by God"; for God cannot be tempted by evil, nor does He himself tempt anyone".

A true man of God must be his semblance. Today, pastors curl and relax their hairs, developing hatred for their nature. Today, a pastor ordered his followers to eat grass when nature has provided fire and ways to hygienically prepared and eat food. Today pastors temp their members and God himself in the guise of miracle.

The work of the true prophet of God will be marked by the good fruit it bears as well as the good fruit it produces. So... what is good fruit?

Galatians 5:22-23,

" But the fruit of the Spirit is love, joy, peace, longsuffering, kindness, goodness, faithfulness, gentleness, self-control. Against such there is no law."

The fruit of the true man of God will reflect goodness, kindness. He must be an exemple to the people but today you see the opposite, instead of rebuking corrupt politicians, they make them their patrons, instead of helping the poor, they psychologically work on them to give to the church.

The true man of God is a valuable source of information, encouragement, as well as idea for a better society. He is a realist, he believe in planning and hard work not miracle, he knew that nature never deviate from it rule without application of force and energy. He is an act of perfection. He is a perfect being.

"Beware of false prophets, who come to you in sheep's clothing, but inwardly they are ravenous wolves" (Matthew 7:15).

Under the plan God has ordained for the church, leadership is a position of humble, loving service. Church leadership is ministry, not management. Those whom God designates as leaders are called not to be governing monarchs, but humble slaves; not slick celebrities, but laboring servants; not instrument of slavery, but force of mental revolution. Those who would lead God's people must above all exemplify sacrifice, devotion, submission, and lowliness.

Jesus Himself gave us the pattern when He stooped to wash His disciples' feet, a task that was customarily done by the lowest of slaves (John 13). If the founder of the Christian faith would do that, no church leader has a right to think of himself as a bigwig, guarded by armed personnel.

Christ defined his pattern of Leadership as servant leadership; which is unlike the world's leadership. And he who wants to lead must serve and the greatest among you, must be your slave.

Omnipotence

> *"Ah, Lord God! Behold, You have made the heavens and the earth by your great power and outstretch arm. There is nothing too hard for you"* Jeremiah 32;17

The omnipotence of God refers to him being "all powerful". This is often conveyed with the phrase "Almighty", as in the Old Testament title "God Almighty" -the conventional translation of the Hebrew title El Shaddai and the title "God the Father Almighty" in the Apostles' Creed. God is able to bring to pass everything that He chooses. He has no external limitations.

Jesus says in Matthew 19:26

> *"...With men this is impossible, but with God all things are possible".*

This concept clarifies as his Omnipotence means power to do all that is intrinsically possible. There is no limit to his power. The book of Job (42:2) says that He can do all things and that nothing can restrain him. Genesis 18:14 simply asks, "Is anything too hard for the LORD?"

A true man of God should bear a semblance of omnipotence. How powerful is your pastor?

To be more certain of your answer, first define what power is. Power is the rate of doing work, the capacity or ability to influence the course of event. A force must be overcome before work can be done, or the curse of event is change.

What work is your pastor doing and what force did he overcome?

1) He build bigger auditorium. He has no force to reckon with while trying to bring this wish to fruition, no law to battle with, and no difficulty in raising cash.

2) He cast out devil. These are pretentious act carried out to create theatrical effect and attract more spectators or members. In reality, they reckoned with no force.

A true man of God must overcome forces to bring things to fruition. Moses overcome the mighty power of the Egyptian government to liberate the Israelites. Elijah overcome the challenge with the prophet of Baal to prove the supremacy of his God over Baal. David conquered goliath and the philistines. What force has your pastor ever overcome?

You can liberate Africa from mental slavery, bringing economic, political, cultural and religious independent by battling with the current system. You could be the next true man of God.

What force is your pastor reckoning with to proof his degree of power? A true man of God must be all powerful. People like Moses, David, Elijah, Elisha, Abraham must be a leader of a people; a race, a country, an empire. A true man of God is a shepherd.

What we called spiritual power is an illusion, the world is made up of matter and energy, energy is what they called spiritual power. This can be proved with a simple experiment. Let a pastor who claims he possesses spiritual power test his power against application of natural laws; technological power and see that which prevail. A pastor should command someone to die, thereafter if the person is not dead; he will shoot the pastor with gun and see which will be killed; spiritual power or technological power.

This is the exact contest Elijah bet with the prophet of Baal, a true demonstration of power.

OMNIPRESENCE

This imply that God is present everywhere and now and that he watches over the affairs of his people
Psalm 33;13-14.
>"The lord look from heaven; he sees all the son of men. From the place of his dwelling he looks on all the inhabitant of the earth".

Jeremiah 23;24.
>"Can anyone hide himself in secret places so I shall not see him?" says the lord; "do I not fill heaven and earth?" Says the lord

Moses was bred in pharaoh's house yet he shared in the suffering of his people. Physically he stays with pharaoh but he was present with the Israelites. This is the true nature of omnipresence. He understands their suffering and at the right time, he rose to free them from bondage.

A true man of God must know your predicament, your financial difficulty, your suffering. He is the one who share in your predicament and suffering and offer direct solution, he is always with you, and he is a friend indeed.

A man of God who neither care, or advice you to invest your first income but rather used it for seed or tithe is a fake man of God for he is not omnipresence. He should have known that the one million naira you have is not even enough to start your desired business, instead he asks for one hundred thousand naira tithe. Such a man of God is not present in your mind.

Proverbs 15;3.

"the eye of the lord are in everyplace, keeping watch on the evil and the good"

Has your man of God ever mobilize against bad leadership? Does your man of God ever preach against brainwashing people to give to church? Ok, if given is noble, does your man of God ever insist you pay your tax, give to the needy, do they ever notice the poverty in the land? Absolutely 'NO' because they are not omnipresence.

Moses noticed the suffering of his people and stood up to liberate them. David noticed the humiliation of his people, he killed Goliath to liberate them. Elijah noticed the humiliation of his God, he challenged the prophet of Baal in a contest to death to salvage the image of his God. These were true men of God, they saw beyond the convenience of their closet.

Today, the acclaimed men of God does not see his member who is being oppressed by his employer or landlord. Today the acclaimed

men of God does not see his member who lacks accommodation. Today the acclaimed men of God does not know the level of corruption in their country nor proffer solution. Today the acclaimed men of God does not know the international politics played against his people; because they lack the omnipresence attribute of God, hence they are not of God.
Luke 17;21.

> "Nor will they say, 'see here!' or see there!' for indeed,
> the kingdom of God is within you"

God is not in church or in your pastor's, you are an embodiment of God. God is with each and every one of us, he is present in everything in the universe. He is omnipresence, He is natural.

OTHER QUALITIES OF A TRUE MAN OF GOD
He led a vision
1 King 13;1-2

> "And behold, a man of God went from Judah to Bethel by the word
> of the lord, and Jeroboam stood by the alter to burn incense.
> Then he cried out against the alter by the word of the lord, and
> said, 'O alter, alter! Thus says the lord: 'Behold, a child, Josiah by
> name, shall be born to the house of David; and on you he shall
> sacrifice the priest of the high place who burn incense
> on you, and men's bones shall be burned on you"

The man of God here leads a vision: the birth of Josiah.
Moses was called the man of God; why? Moses was called to lead

the children of Israel out of Egypt The bible often uses sheep and the shepherd when describing the leader and the lead. There must be a shepherd to lead the flock lest they wander away. Moses was leading a revolution, he possessed the spirit of revolution right from youth, he demonstrated this when he killed an Egyptian who fought with a Jew. He liberates his people from slavery.

What are the problems of your society and what measure is your pastor adopting to solve these problems. Ask this question and provide the answer, then you will realize that you have been under bondage. What is your church mission?

Some claim they give wealth, how, through divine blessing, favor, prayer and so on. When God fed the Israelites, the manner fell from heaven, when Jesus fed thousands of people, it happened instantly after prayer, when Moses parted the red sea for his people to pass to safety, it happened instantly, but when your church is giving wealth, you have to wait for God's visitation.

There are so many problems in the society ranging from poverty, unemployment, human right abuse etc. what has your church done to liberate any of this societal problem. They may argue that it is not their responsibility, what is the church responsibility then? The churches in Africa are not adding value to Africa; rather they contributed in dragging Africa deep into mental slavery.

All 'liberated' men should be men of God but when the Bible speaks of a man of God it speaks of someone called for a specific purpose, to lead a vision. Moses was called to bring forth the children of Israel out of Egypt. What was your pastor called to do? Probably to lead you to heaven, that's pure lie. But the question is 'Men of God, how can you tell'?

Simple, ask what is the mission of the church, how exactly will such mission impact on the life of the people and the society as a whole. Most churches does not have mission, the ones that have are blur, vague, non-beneficiary and ambiguous. They are simply a statement written on a piece of paper which if practiced, will never add value to the people's lives. This will tell you if the founder, your pastor is a true man of God.

The assumption of blessing from God through your pastor is an illusion, the promise of good fortune from God by your pastor is manipulation, and the hope of a miracle through your pastor is bondage.

The nationalist movement of the pre-independent Africa and their leaders were more of God than the present day prophets and pastors. Martin Luther king was more of God than many pastors of today. Ojukwu of eastern Nigeria was more of God than many present day bishop, or acclaimed God's generals.

He must be a thought leader

Christianity today is so refine to accommodate all sort of things, some encourage women to come to church without pant and bra to ensure that the holy spirit pass through them, other prefer trouser and mini skirt for their female congregation, others makes you believed in 'holy water' and 'holy handkerchief' to save you. Today Christianity gives the society what they want not what is morally, culturally, economically and technically good.

What does your church symbolize?

What does a pastor who owns an expensive school symbolize, other than the ideology of "school is not for the poor"?

What does a pastor who owns a private jet symbolize other than the fact that church is a lucrative business?

What does a pastor or church who received money for counseling and blessing symbolize, other than a consultancy firm?

I had preachers lie to me, right to my face, and when I found out it didn't even bother them, no apology. What we have today in the church is a lot of Mummy, Daddy, and some sort of men that called themselves men of God and it shows in their ministry.

Most churches built school training young men on how to be a man of God but to no avail; because they are not called and if you're not called it does not work. Most of the pulpits in Africa are being filled by men that want to be there, or think they are called. And when you have men in the ministry who are not called, the respect of the position is gone because they do not have what it takes to be a pastor. They are not men of God.

What ideology does your pastor represent? What message apart from the regular prosperity message and promises of blessing and miracles?

"God will bless someone today" the pastor proclaimed, "Amen" thundered the ignorant congregation.

How will God bless you without you setting goals, backing the goal with motive, planning and executing it? There is nothing as divine favor. Your mind can only attract only what you desire or related issue. Your mind is God's working tool in you.

Moses was a taught leader, he plan and executes the liberation of his people from Egypt. He was a true man of God.

Abraham established the concept of God and gives birth to religion. He was a taught leader, a true man of God.

David was a taught leader, he believed in the superiority of the Jews above all race.

What exactly does your church represent? What message are they giving you? Anything contrary to true liberation is not of God.

He who is not a thought leader is not of God.

He shows the right way

"...See, here is water. What hinders me from being baptized?" Acts 8:36

The above question shows an eager heart, someone desperate, and someone in total confirmation of what he believed. The question was asked by an Ethiopian court official in the first century. Who was reading the book of the prophets but did not understand it, he became confused and frustrated. Although he spends hours reading it, the real meaning is not there.

Lead by the Holy Spirit, a young and vibrant Christian brother named Philip, joined him in his chariot and knowing fully well that although this Eunuch is reading, that he does not understand it, he asked him:

Do you understand what you are reading?

Wholeheartedly, the Eunuch answered him; how can I? Unless someone guide me; the bible said he desired Philip that he would come up and sit with him and pleaded that Philip explain it to him.

Philip opened his mouth wide and explains everything to him-the gospel. Deeply touched to the heart by what he had learned from the scripture, the Ethiopian Eunuch on seeing a body of water, yearned and cried out:

"...*See, here is water. What hinders me from being baptized? Acts 8:36.*

Today, many people are obviously reading the bible without understanding, so they ask their pastor for explanations but the false men of God gave them the following explanations;

1) You will only receive blessing from God if you pay your tithe and offering, for you cannot cheat God and expect good things.
2) All sickness is of the devil, so instead of hospital when sick, go for prayers.
3) That whatever station you find yourself in life was ordained by God to be so; God's divine plan.
4) That poverty and wealth are of God and has nothing to do with your mental ability.
5) That prayer solves all problems.
6) That God is good all the time, he never endorse slavery, rape, human sacrifice, infant murder, genocide and animal mishandling.
7) That even when you murdered someone today and accept Christ tomorrow, your sin is wipe out.
8) That all your problems is gone in Jesus name today.

They are lies, lies and lies to keep the congregation chain.

A true man of God shows and leads the right way. This obviously shows that, there is a wrong way. The above mentioned answers which are currently obtainable in churches today are the wrong ways.

He always warns of the wrong way and leads his flock to the right way

A true man of God will tell you that blessing come from within, they will encourage you to work hard and never rely on them for blessing, they inform you that sickness are caused by bacteria and deficiency, he will encourage you to plan and invest your money wisely and advice you to visit the hospital when sick.

If your pastor ever tells you that he will bless you or actually carry out an act of blessing or demanded money for any of his services, such a pastor is not of God.

A true man of God will encourage you to visit the hospital when sick and pray for you in the hospital, he will not pretend to be a doctor, a midwife, a pastor, a consultant, an arbitrator all at once. He will encourage you to visit hospital for child delivery.

A Christian is a believer, who keeps the commandment of love of God and man. You cannot say you love men and cheat them or lie to them or fool them or control them to your own advantage. You cannot mislead your people and claim to be a man of God.

Finally, I do not say pastors should be beggarly; they should not obtain their wealth through manipulation and deceit. Many Christians are multi-millionaires from hard work. Many pastors get fantastic gifts (cars, cheque, etc.) and that is good if the gift is not given in anticipation of expected return inform of blessing or miracle or as a gift for a miracle.

During marriage ceremony, you give gift to the bride and groom without expecting anything back from them. Given to a pastor in anticipation of result, sowing of seed in anticipation of a reward wrong.

Many are poor and giving to the rich pastors because of expectation of return in a thousand fold. Is God a company that you are investing in? This trend ought to stop. Those who gives to pastors do so because they believe the pastor is responsible for their success, this is lie. They give in fearful faith.

I hope you get my point now. That is how I define a true man of God; love from the shepherd to the sheep.

You can know the man of God because he can show you the way you should go just as the servant of Saul affirmed;

I Sam. 9:6

> *"And he said to him, "Look now, there is in this city a man of God and he is an honorable man; all that he says surely comes to pass. So let us go there; perhaps he can show us the way that we should go."*

He said this because he is fully aware that a man of God could give them directions; the right way to follow...." A man of God today is someone who has a message from God and can show you the way you should go and afraid of no one. He stands on the path of truth and love. He is a realist.

Many preachers today are afraid to lose their large congregation, modest clothing, and celebrity life style. Therefore, they prefer brainwashing the people instead of telling them the truth, but true man of God loves his people and knows where the other way leads, to destruction, to mental slavery, to intellectual bondage, to poverty, to low standard of living.

Tell them that magic rephrase 'miracle' does not exist, tell them that nature God has given them everything they need to survive so all what they need is to explore, tell them that creativity, productivity, science and technology reduces poverty, tell them that God is nature. That's your duty as a true man of God.

Churches are falling apart as it seems because preachers are spineless and afraid to make a stand against religious dependence, corruption, mental slavery, tribalism. The sources of their members income is none of their business.

Where are the men of God like Moses, who affirmed; "Who is on the Lord's side?" or the Elijah's who stood against the false prophets? I am on the lord side so I kick against economic, political, cultural, religious and technological dependency of Africa.

He is not there for the money

"For the love of money is a root of all kinds of evil, for which some have strayed from the faith in their greediness, and pierced themselves through with many sorrows. But you, O man of God, flee these things and pursue righteousness, godliness, faith, love, patience, gentleness". 1 Timothy 6:10-11

Many in their bid, quest to have money have wandered away from the truth and the right way, and have pierced their hearts with sorrows. That is the major chaos and discord in the church today. The so-called men of God have deviated and wandered away from the truth, they are in the quest for money.

Want to spot a true man of God? Look at his lifestyle. I have known so-called pastors who live like kings but cannot afford to support the poor, charge the highest fee in their schools, train his son to take over the empire and deceive people to sow seed and wait for reaping without they themselves sowing any outside their church. They go around with armed security.

Many families have been destroyed because of church doctrines that rob the poor to pay the rich pastor. The bible clearly warns that men of God should stay away from money which currently, they are not doing. They disobey the bible; therefore they are false prophets, mere religious leaders.

CHAPTER TWO

TRUE MEN OF GOD

A BRIEF LIFETIME ACT OF
BIBLICAL MEN OF GOD

From biblical view, the following people were at one point called men of God and their lifestyles co-incide with the attribute of God as we previously stated;

David

Nehemiah 12;24

> 'And the heads of the levites were Hashabiah, Sherebiah, and Jeshua the son of Kadmiel, with their brothers across from them, to praise and gives thanks, group alternating with group, according to the command of David the man of God'

David was the last son of his parents who kept the flocks for his family. He took food to his elder brothers on battle ground, saw another race humiliating his people, he decided to liberated his people from shame.

He creates history by killing Goliath whose only crime was to humiliate it people. Is it not a sin to kill? For God, it was not a sin because he killed to protect his people who claimed to be God choosing.

A true man of God just as the United States government; Gods own state, never allowed any person, organization or nation to humiliate her people and go scot free. That was what David did, that's what America is doing. What of Africa? Answer for yourself.

David intended killing Nabal for refusing to offer him something in return for his good nature toward his sheep's and the shepherd. A true man of God is never a subordinate, he never forgive those who offend him. This quality is also found in Elisha when he curses the forty two kids that mock him. These were men of God.

1 Samuel 22;1-2. David gathered an army and fight. You don't fight the devil by casting and binding, you fight the devil with real weapons because the devil is human like you.

He was ordained king over Judah, then over Israel and Judah, he guided and led his people to many victories in war, he was provident. He showed love to his people by fighting for them not against them. He was omnipotent when he single handedly killed goliath, which was an all-powerful act.

David was never a prophet neither did he perform any miracle but the bible called him "man of God" He was an embodiment of Love for his people, he put his life at risk for his people.

Moses

Deuteronomy 33;1,

> "Now this is the blessing with which Moses the man of God blessed the children of Israel before his death"

Born around 1391BC at the time Hebrews were slaves in Egypt, the glowing population of the Jew threatened pharaoh, so he ordered for the execution of all new born male. He was saved by his mother, Picked and raised in pharaohs' house, he never forgot he was a Hebrew.

Moses was a great leader and lawgiver of the Hebrew. After killing an Egyptian for the sake of the Jews (Exodus 3;11-12), he escaped to Midian, returned back to Egypt to lead a revolution that freed his people from bondage.

He killed thousands of Egyptians on the process and finally liberated the Israelite from Egypt.

He turn Egyptian waters to blood (Exodus 7;20) this is similar to freezing the asset of your enemy.

He converted dust to lice (Exodus 8;17) and swamp of flies (Exodus 8;24). This is similar to the release of biological weapon on your enemy. Many have been unleashed in Africa.

Moses attacks with chemical and biological weapon until the Israelite were set free. He was similar to the independent movement leaders in Africa.

He led a vision, the liberation of the Israelites from Egypt. He displayed love for his people when he killed an Egyptian that fought with his fellow Jew. He carried out an all-powerful act by confronting pharaoh to let his people go, an omnipotent act. Moses was a revolutionary leader.

His mission was to lead the Israelites out of Egypt and he die just after fulfilling the mission.

Elijah

1 King 17;18,

> "So she said to Elijah, "What have I to do with you, O man of God? Have you come to me to bring my sin to remembrance, and to kill my son?"

He was a true man of God because all his prophesies came to fulfillment. Unlike the current crops of Men of God we have in Nigeria who prophesies that President Jonathan will be re-elected, but he failed. Elijah's prophesy never cease to come to fulfillment, even once.

He said there will be no rain for years and there was no rain for years

(1 king 17;1) He told the widow that camped him that her food will never run dry and so it was (1 king 17;17-24)

He stood in an open contest with the prophet of Baal challenging them to the supremacy of his God, he showed the right way, he wasn't afraid to point out the way and even challenge in a contest of death. Have your pastor ever taken such bold steps, of course no.

Elijah prophesy fulfilled again in 2 king 9;35-37. Only a true man of God can carry out such challenges, to this I challenge all acclaimed men of God in Nigeria to proof that science is the true study of God and technology is the only miracle.

Let 'the religious men of God' gather in a stadium, I will also gather 'the true men of God'. Let them pray for their God to strike us dead, then with the permission and supply from the government, we will unleash full magazine of an AK47 gun on them and see which will kill. This will verify which is powerful between the God of the bible and koran and that of science and technology.

NATO killed the prophet of Libya, Belgium killed the prophet of D R Congo. How long shall they kill our true prophets?

True men of God are true semblance of God. They are merciless, jealous and protective of their own even when they commit the worst crime. David killed Uriah to take his wife and God forgave him but instead killed the child that was born through that affair, that's God.

Elijah was a true man of God.

Elisha - 2 King 4;1-7

"A certain woman of the wives of the sons of the prophets cried out to Elisha, saying....Then she came and told the man of God. And he said, "Go, sell the oil and pay your debt; and you and your sons live on the rest."

The first thing Elisha did after receiving the mantle of Elijah was to divide river Jordan to enable him go back, then he blessed a body of water.

On his way, forty two children mocked him and he cursed them, behold two she bears out of the wood killed the forty two children 2 king 2;11-25

That's exactly what a true man of God does, killed any nation that mock her nation, any people that mock her people. That was exactly why David killed Goliath. The bible gives us direction.

All the miracle Elisha did were instant 2 kings 4;1-44

In 2 kings 4;42 a man brought bread of first fruit to Elisha, twenty loaves of barley and full ears of corn but Elisha say "give to the people that they may eat" which of the acclaimed men of God, our so called daddies and mummies can do this, give the offering and tithe money to the people instead of himself?

2 Kings 5:8 'So it was when Elisha the man of God heard that the king of Israel had torn his robes, that he sent to the king, saying, "Why have you torn your robes? Please let him comes to me, and he shall know that there is a prophet in Israel."

Samuel
1 Samuel 9;5-19

"When they had come to the land of Zuph, saul said to his servant who

*was with him, "Come, let us return, lest my father cease caring about
the donkeys and become worried about us" And he said to him,,
"Look now, there is in this city a man of God, and he is
an honorable man; all that he says surely comes to pass.
So let us go there. Perhaps he can show us the way that we should go"
.....so they went up to the city. As they were coming into the city,
there was Samuel, coming out toward them on his way
up to the high place...Samuel answer Saul and said "I am the seer.
Go up before me to the high place, for you shall eat with me
today; and tomorrow I will let you go and will tell you
all that is in your heart"*

There was a time the Israelites demanded for a king instead of a judge and Samuel granted the wish of the people. All true leaders, true men of God live to fulfill the wish of the people. 1 Sam 8:4-22.

During the campaign against the Amalekites, King Saul spared Agag, the king of the Amalekites, and the best of their livestock. Saul tell Samuel that he spared the choice of the Amalekites' sheep and oxen, intending to sacrifice the livestock to the Lord. This was in violation of the Lord's command, as pronounced by Samuel, to "... utterly destroy all that they have, and spare them not; but slay both men and women, infant and suckling, ox and sheep, camels and assess" (1 Samuel 15:3). Samuel confronts Saul for his disobedience and tell him that God made him king, and God can unmake him king. Samuel then proceeded to execute Agag. Saul never saw Samuel alive again. Samuel was a king maker, a ruler of kings, a policy maker. Like other true men of God, he was a liberator, a decision maker

→ TRUE MEN OF GOD?

Others
1 Timothy 6:10-11

"For the love of money is a root of all kinds of evil, for which some have strayed from the faith in their greediness, and pierced themselves through with many sorrows. But you, O man of God, flee these things and pursue righteousness, godliness, faith, love, patience, gentleness.

2 king 4;42, Some gift were given to Elisha as a man of God instead he ordered that the gifts should be given to those who have less. Today such never happen; those who gives scholarships in their school are doing so because they actually loose nothing. They can only loose if they gives the scholarship in another school.

All the biblical men of God share the following in common.
1) They all fight for the liberation of their people or believe.
2) They love only their people.
3) Most of them were not religious leaders.
4) They all killed for the liberation of their people.

PAST AFRICAN MEN OF GOD AND THEIR ATTRIBUTE
Patrice Lumumba

A tall, thin, intense man, born a member of the small Batatela tribe in kasai province in 1925. He was the first prime minister of Congo, a true man of God, an African savior

During Congo's independence on 30thJune 1960, he delivered the following speech

Men, and women of the Congo,

Victorious independence fighters,

I salute you in the name of the Congolese Government.

I ask all of you, my friends, who tirelessly fought in our ranks, to mark this June 30, 1960, as an illustrious date that will be ever engraved in your hearts, a date whose meaning you will proudly explain to your children, so that they in turn might relate to their grandchildren and great-grandchildren the glorious history of our struggle for freedom.

Although this independence of the Congo is being proclaimed today by agreement with Belgium, an amicable country, with which we are on equal terms, no Congolese will ever forget that independence was won in struggle, a persevering and inspired struggle carried on from day to day, a struggle, in which we were undaunted by privation or suffering and stinted neither strength nor blood.

It was filled with tears, fire and blood. We are deeply proud of our struggle, because it was just and noble, indispensable in putting an end to the humiliating bondage forced upon us.

That was our lot for the eighty years of colonial rule and our wounds are too fresh and much too painful to be forgotten.

We have experienced forced labour in exchange for pay that did not allow us to satisfy our hunger, to clothe ourselves, to have decent lodgings or to bring up our children as dearly loved ones.

Morning, noon and night we were subjected to jeers, insults and blows because we were "Negroes". Who will ever forget that the black was addressed as "tu", not because he was a friend, but because the polite "vous" was reserved for the white man?

We have seen our lands seized in the name of ostensibly just laws, which gave recognition only to the right of might.

We have not forgotten that the law was never the same for the white and the black, that it was lenient to the ones, and cruel and inhuman to the others.

We have experienced the atrocious sufferings, being persecuted for political convictions and religious beliefs, and exiled from our native land: our lot was worse than death itself.

We have not forgotten that in the cities the mansions were for the whites and the tumbledown huts for the blacks; that a black was not admitted to the cinemas, restaurants and shops set aside for "Europeans"; that a black travelled in the holds, under the feet of the whites in their luxury cabins.

Who will ever forget the shootings which killed so many of our brothers, or the cells into which were mercilessly thrown those who no longer wished to submit to the regime of injustice, oppression and exploitation used by the colonialists as a tool of their domination?

All that, my brothers, brought us untold suffering. But we, who were elected by the votes of your representatives, representatives of the people, to guide our native land, we, who have suffered in body and soul from the colonial oppression, we tell you that henceforth all that is finished.

The Republic of the Congo has been proclaimed and our beloved country's future is now in the hands of its own people.

Brothers, let us commence together a new struggle, a sublime struggle that will lead our country to peace, prosperity and greatness.

Together we shall establish social justice and ensure for every man a fair remuneration for his labour.

We shall show the world what the black man can do when working in liberty, and we shall make Congo the pride of Africa.

We shall see to it that the lands of our native country truly benefit its children.

We shall revise all the old laws and make new laws that will be just and noble.

We shall stop the persecution of free thought. We shall see to it that all citizens enjoy to the fullest extent the basic freedoms provided by the Declaration of Human Rights.

We shall eradicate all discrimination, whatever its origin, and we shall ensure for everyone a station in life befitting his human dignity and worthy of his labour and loyalty to the country.

We shall institute in the country a peace resting not on guns and bayonets but on concord and goodwill.

And in all this, my dear compatriots, we can rely not only on our own enormous forces and immense wealth, but also on the assistance of the numerous foreign states, whose co-operation we shall accept when it is not aimed at imposing upon us an alien policy, but is given in a spirit of friendship.

Even Belgium, which has finally learned the lesson of history and need no longer try to oppose our independence, is prepared to give us its aid and friendship; for that end an agreement has just been signed between our two equal and independent countries. I am sure that this co-operation will benefit both countries. For our part, we shall, while remaining vigilant, try to observe the engagements we have freely made.

Thus, both in the internal and external spheres, the new Congo being created by my government will be rich, free and prosperous. But to attain our goal without delay, I ask all of you, legislators and citizens of the Congo, to give us all the help you can.

I ask you all to sink your tribal quarrels: they weaken us and may cause us to be despised abroad.

I ask you all not to shrink from any sacrifice for the sake of ensuring the success of our grand undertaking.

Finally, I ask you unconditionally to protect the life and property of fellow-citizens and foreigners who have settled in our country; if the conduct of these foreigners leaves much to be desired, our Justice will promptly expel them from the territory of the republic; if, on the contrary, their conduct is good, they must be left in peace, for they, are also working for our country's prosperity.

The Congo's independence is a decisive step towards the liberation of the whole African continent.

Our government, a government of national and popular unity, will serve its country.

I call on all Congolese citizens, men, women and children, to set themselves resolutely to the task of creating a national economy and ensuring our economic independence.

Eternal glory to the fighters for national liberation!

Long live independence and African unity!
Long live the independent and sovereign Congo!

Lumumba was all powerful; he founded The Mouvement National Congolais, MNC and declared: "The$_2$ mouvement National Congolais has as its basic aim the liberation of the Congolese people from the colonial regime...we wish to bid farewell to the old regime, this regime of subjection...Africa is engaged in a merciless struggle for its liberation against the colonizer" and he succeeded because nothing can stand between him and his wish as a true man of God.

This was what Moses did, he overcame the Egyptian government to free the Jews.

Power is the ability to alter event, a force must be subdued for work to be done and that force was the Belgium government. Unlike many acclaimed men of God who encountered no force in their pursuit. That was exactly what lumumba did, he overcame force.

The independent movement in Congo was not an easy task as we may assume today just as the elimination of neo-colonialism and mental slavery is not an easy task but will usher in a new man of God in the person of the leaders of such movement and true believers in the followers.

God is able to bring to pass everything that He chooses. He has no external limitations. So was Patrice Lumumba, he brought about the political independence of Congo, a noble cause he chooses.

A true man of God should beer a semblance of omnipotent. How powerful is your pastor?

What work is your pastor doing and what force did he overcome?

1) He build bigger auditorium. He has no force to reckon with while trying to bring this wish to fruition. The finance comes from the members.

2) He cast out devil. These are pretentious act carried out to create theatrical mood and attract more spectators or members. In reality, they reckoned with no force. What they call spiritual force are in reality natural forces such as gravity.

3) There is no government restriction for the establishment of churches, no licensing is required and no tax is imposed, just CAC registration.

Patrice Lumumba overcame the colonial force and brought independence to Congo, this is true omnipotence. He overcames forces. That is true definition of power.

Attempt to split your country, attempt to stop trade imbalance, attempt to stop importation of fuel and refine all our natural resources, attempt to introduce a single gold African currency, attempt to stop mental slavery, attempt to stop dependency of Africa, attempt to stop neo-colonialism, attempt to create Africa true nations base on the wish and aspiration of the people etc. and you will understand the true meaning of omnipotence.

Lumumba led the Congolese independent movement from Belgium just as Moses lead the Israelites out of Egypt to their independent land. Though he embraces Russia and UN at various stages and lack tact in his execution, which betrayed the very essence of true independence, he portrays the quality of a true man of God by leading a mission. Shemaiah equally led a mission. Compare him to your man of God who has no vision. Some churches has mission and vision statement, read them and you will notice they did not entail the liberation of the people or design to add real value to the life of the people.

How can a churche's vision be 5,000,000 adult members in 5 years? This is about expansion and profit, the character of business. A true man of God must not always be a preacher, David, Moses, Shemaiah were not preachers

The independence speech was a display of solidarity and passionate love for his people. Lumumba refused to be coax by the Belgium rather choose to show his resentment toward the treatment Belgium emitted to his people. He was an epitome of love for his Congolese people. Moses displayed love to the Israelites, his people not the Egyptians when he killed the Egyptian.

God himself display his love mostly to his choosing people. Therefore a true man of God must do the same; Love only his people.

1) Secondary schools and universities established by your church must charge members no or less fee than they charge others and such fee must be minimal. This is an act of love a true man of God must display to his people. If your pastor is not doing it, he is not of God.

2) Has your church ever bought food items and share to her poor members?

3) What actual value does your church add to your life apart from baseless hope?

A true man of God, just as God is independent. He does not create or encourage dependency, not even in God. He propagates the ideology of political, economic, cultural, religious and technological independence.

Lumumba was an advocate of political and economic independence, a true man of God.

Gods independence is also refers to God's sovereignty, it is God's self-existence and self-sufficiency. A leader that advocates self-sufficience, self-existence, self-determination, self-independence is a true man of God.

We all know today that people rely on religious leaders for virtually everything, some worship their pastors. Will an independent God want you to be dependent on mere mortal for yours spiritual and physical need?

Veracity means telling truth. Read Patrice lumumba independence day speech, it is raw truth without fear, it is uncensored.

Marcus Garvey
QUOTES BY GARVEY$_3$

> "Our success educationally, industrially, politically is based upon the protection of a nation founded by ourselves and that nation can be nowhere else but in Africa".
>
> "A people without the past knowledge of their past history, origin and culture is like a tree without root"

> "The black skin is not a make of shame, but rather
> a glorious symbol of national greatness"
> "Chance has never get satisfy the hope of a suffering people"

> "Liberate the minds of men and ultimately you
> will liberate the body of men"

> "I know no national boundary where the negro is concern.
> The whole world is my province until Africa is free"
> "There shall be no solution to the race problem until you,
> yourself strike the blow of liberty"

Marcus Garvey and his organization, the Universal Negro Improvement Association (UNIA), represent the largest mass movement in African-American history. Proclaiming a Black Nationalist "Back to Africa" message, Garvey and the UNIA established 700 branches in thirty-eight states by the early 1920s. While chapters existed in the larger urban areas such as New York, Chicago, and Los Angeles, Garvey's message reached into small towns across the country as well. Later groups such as Father Divine's Universal Peace Mission Movement and the Nation of Islam drew members and philosophy from Garvey's organization, and the UNIA's appeal and influence were felt not only in America but in Canada, the Caribbean, and throughout Africa.

Garvey's philosophy and organization had a rich religious component that he blended with the political and economic aspects.

Considering the strong political and economic black nationalism of

Garvey's movement, it may seem odd to include an essay on him in a Web-site on religion in America. However, his philosophy and organization had a rich religious component that he blended with the political and economic aspects. Garvey himself claimed that his "Declaration of Rights of the Negro Peoples of the World," along with the Bible, served as "the Holy Writ for our Negro Race." He stated clearly that "as we pray to Almighty God to save us through his Holy Words so shall we with confidence in ourselves follow the sentiment of the Declaration of Rights and carve our way to liberty." For Garvey, it was no less than the will of God for black people to be free to determine their own destiny. His organization took as its motto "One God! One Aim! One Destiny!" and looked to the literal fulfillment of Psalm 68:31:

"Princes shall come out of Egypt: Ethiopia shall soon stretch forth her hands unto God."

Garvey was born in 1887 in St. Anne's Bay, Jamaica. Due to the economic hardship of his family, he left school at age fourteen and learned the printing and newspaper business. He became interested in politics and soon got involved in projects aimed at helping those on the bottom of society. Unsatisfied with his work, he travelled to London in 1912 and stayed in England for two years. During this time he paid close attention to the controversy between Ireland and England concerning Ireland's independence. He was also exposed to the ideas and writings of a group of black colonial writers that came together in London around the African Times and Orient Review. Nationalism in both Ireland and Africa along with ideas such as race conservation undoubtedly had an impact on Garvey.

However, he later remembered that the most influential experience of his stay in London was reading Booker T. Washington's autobiography Up from Slavery. Washington believed African Americans needed to improve themselves first, showing whites in America that they deserved equal rights. Although politically involved behind the scenes, Washington repeatedly claimed that African Americans would not benefit from political activism and started an industrial training school in Alabama that embodied his own philosophy of self-help. Garvey embraced Washington's ideas and returned to Jamaica in 1914 to found the UNIA with the motto "One God! One Aim! One Destiny!"

Initially he kept very much in line with Washington by encouraging his fellow Jamaicans of African descent to work hard, demonstrate good morals and a strong character, and not worry about politics as a tool to advance their cause. Garvey did not make much headway in Jamaica and decided to visit America in order to meet Booker T. Washington and learn more about the situation of African Americans. By the time Garvey arrived in America in 1916, Washington had died, but Garvey decided to travel around the country and observe African Americans and their struggle for equal rights.

What Garvey saw was a shifting population and a diminishing hope in Jim Crow's demise. African Americans were moving in large numbers out of the rural South and into the urban areas of both

North and South. As World War One came to an end, disillusionment was beginning to take hold. Not only was the optimism in the continuing improvement of humanity and society broken apart, but so was any hope on the part of African Americans that they would gain the rights enjoyed by every white American citizen. African Americans had served in large numbers in the war, and many expected some kind of respect and acknowledgment that they too were equal citizens. Indeed, World War One was the perfect opportunity for African Americans to fulfill Booker T. Washington's requirement for equality and freedom. Through dedicated service in the armed forces, they could prove their worth and showed they deserved the same rights as whites. However, as black soldiers returned from the war, more African Americans moved into the urban areas, racial tensions grew. Between 1917 and 1919 race riots erupted in East St. Louis, Chicago, Tulsa, and other cities, demonstrating that whites did not intend to treat African Americans any differently than they had before the war.

After surveying the racial situation in America, Garvey was convinced that integration would never happen and that only economic, political, and cultural success on the part of African Americans would bring about equality and respect.(and he was right, segregation will have been solved by segregation) With this goal he established the headquarters of the UNIA in New York in 1917 and began to spread a message of black nationalism and the eventual return to Africa of all people of African descent. His brand of Black Nationalism had three components, pride in the African cultural heritage, and complete autonomy. Garvey believed people of African descent could establish a great independent nation in their ancient homeland of Africa. He took the self-help message of Washington and adapted it to the situation he saw in America, taking a somewhat individualistic, integrationist philosophy and turning it into a more corporate, politically-minded, nation-building message.

In 1919 Garvey purchased an auditorium in Harlem and named it Liberty Hall. There he held nightly meetings to get his message out, sometimes to an audience of six thousand. In 1918 he began a newspaper, Negro World, which by 1920 had a circulation somewhere between 50,000 and 200,000. Membership in the UNIA is difficult to assess. At one point, Garvey claimed to have six million members. That figure is most likely inflated. However, it is beyond dispute that millions were involved and directly affected by Garvey and his message.

To promote unity, Garvey encouraged African Americans to be concerned with themselves first. He stated after World War One that "the first dying that is to be done by the black man in the future will be done to make himself free. And then when we are finished, if we have any charity to bestow, we may die for the white man. But as for me, I think I have stopped dying for him." Black people had to do the work that success and independence demanded, and, most important, they had to do that work for themselves. "If you want liberty," claimed Garvey to a meeting held in 1921, "you yourselves must strike the blow. If you must be free, you must become so through your own effort."

But Garvey knew African Americans would not take action if they did not change their perceptions. He hammered home the idea of racial pride by celebrating the African past and encouraging African Americans to be proud of their heritage and proud of the way they looked. Garvey proclaimed "black is beautiful" long before it became popular in the 1960s. He wanted African Americans to see themselves as members of a mighty race. "We must calonize our own saints, create our own martyrs, and elevate to positions of fame, honor black men and women who have made their distinct contributions to our racial history." He encouraged parents to give their children "dolls that look like them to play with and cuddle," he did not want black people thinks of themselves in a defeated way. "I am the equal of any white man; I want you to feel the same way."

Garvey organized his group in a way that made those sentiments visible. He created an African Legion that dressed in military garb, uniformed matching bands, and other auxiliary groups such as the Black Cross Nurses.

Marcus Garvey with Potentate Gabriel M. Johnson of Liberia, Supreme Deputy G.O. Marke of Sierra Leone, and other UNIA leaders review the parade opening the 1922 UNIA convention,

He was elected in 1920 as provisional President of Africa by the members of the UNIA and dressed in a military uniform with a plumed hat. At the UNIA's First International Convention in 1920, people lined the street of Harlem to watch Garvey and his followers, dressed in their military outfits, match to their meeting under banners that read "We Want a Black Civilization" and "Africa Must Be Free." All the pomp brought Garvey ridicule from mainstream

African-American leaders, but it also served to inspire many African Americans who had never seen black people so bold and daring.

While racial pride and unity played important roles in Garvey's black nationalism, he touted capitalism as the tool that would establish African Americans as an independent group. His message has been called the evangel of black success, for he believed economic success was the quickest and most effective way to independence. Interestingly enough, it was white America that served as a prime example of what blacks could accomplish. "Until you produce what the white man has produced," he claimed, "you will not be his equal."

In 1919 he established the Negro Factories Corporation and offered stock for African Americans to buy. He wanted to produce everything that a nation needed so that African Americans could completely rely on their own efforts. At one point the corporation operated three grocery stores, two restaurants, a printing plant, a steam laundry, and owned several buildings and trucks in New York City alone. His most famous economic venture was a shipping company known as the Black Star Line, a counterpart to a white-owned company called the White Star Line. Garvey started the shipping company in 1919 as a way to promote trade but also to transport passengers to Africa. He believed it could also serve as an important and tangible sign of black success. However the shipping company eventually failed due to expensive repairs, mismanagement, and corruption.

With all his talk of a mighty race that would one day rule Africa, it would have been foolish for Garvey to underestimate the power of religion, particularly Christianity, within the African-American community. The churches served as the only arena in which African Americans exercised full control. Not only did they serve as houses of worship but also as meeting places that dealt with social, economic, and political issues. Pastors were the most powerful people in the community for they influenced and controlled the community's most important institution. Garvey knew the important place religion held, he worked hard to recruit pastors into his organization. He enjoyed tremendous success at winning over leaders from almost every denomination. One of those clergymen, George Alexander McGuire, an Episcopalian, was elected chaplain-general of the UNIA in 1920. McGuire wrote the UNIA's official liturgy, the "Universal Negro Ritual" and the "Universal Negro Catechism" that set forth the teachings of the UNIA. He attempted to shape the UNIA into a Christian black-nationalist organization. Garvey, however, did not want the organization to take on the trappings of one particular denomination, he did not want to offend any of its members. McGuire left UNIA in 1921 to begin his own church, the African Orthodox Church, a black-nationalist neo-Anglican denomination that kept close ties with the UNIA.

The UNIA meetings at Liberty Hall in Harlem were rich with religious ritual and language, as Randall Burkett points out in his book Black Redemption: Churchmen Speak for the Garvey Movement. Even though Garvey rejected McGuire's effort to transform the UNIA into a black-nationalist Christian denomination, he blended these two traditions in his message and

in the form of his UNIA meetings. A typical meeting followed this order:
>The hymn "Shine On, Eternal Light," written specifically for the UNIA by its music director
>
>A reading of Psalm 68:31: "Princes shall come out of Egypt: Ethiopia shall soon stretch forth her hands unto God."
>
>The official opening hymn "From Greenland's Icy Mountains," stating a commitment to the Christianization of Africa
>
>Recitation of the official motto, "One God! One Aim! One Destiny!"
>
>"The Lord's Prayer" and other prayers spoken by the chaplain
>
>A sermon or some brief remarks
>
>The business meeting

The closing hymn, either "Onward Christian Soldiers" or the UNIA's national anthem,

The "Universal Negro Anthem."

Garvey's black nationalism blended with his Christian outlook rather dramatically when he claimed that African Americans should view God "through our own spectacles." If whites could view God as white, then blacks could view God as black. In 1924 the convention canonized Jesus Christ as a "Black Man of Sorrows" and the Virgin Mary as a "Black Madonna." Garvey used that image as an inspiration to succeed in this life, for African Americans needed to worship a God that understood their plight, understood their suffering, and would help them overcome their present state.

Garvey was not interested in promoting hope in the afterlife. Success in this life was the key. Achieving economic, cultural, social, and political success would free African Americans in this life. The afterlife would take care of itself. Perhaps Garvey's greatest genius was taking that message of material, social, and political success and transforming it into a religious message, one that could lead to 'conversion,' one that did not challenge the basic doctrines of his followers but incorporated them into the whole of his vision. One of Garvey's top ministers gave witness to the powerful effect of that message when he claimed in 1920, "I feel that I am a full-fledged minister of the African gospel."

Garvey's message of Black Nationalism and a free black Africa met considerable resistance from other African-American leaders. W.E.B. DuBois and James Weldon Johnson of the NAACP, and Chandler Owen and A. Philip Randolph of the publication Messenger, had their doubts about Garvey. By 1922 his rhetoric shifted away from a confrontational stance against white America to a position of separatism mixed with just enough cooperation. He applauded whites who promoted the idea of sending African Americans back to Africa. He even met with a prominent leader of the Ku Klux Klan in Atlanta in 1922 to discuss their views on miscegenation and social equality. That meeting only gave more fuel to his critics. In 1924 DuBois claimed that "Marcus Garvey is the most dangerous enemy of the Negro race in America and in the world." Owen and Randolph, whose paper saw the race issue as one of class more than skin color, called Garvey the "messenger boy of the Klan" and a "Supreme Negro Jamaican jackass" while labeling his organization the "Uninformed Negroes Infamous Association."

The federal government also took an interest in Garvey and in 1922 indicted him for mail fraud. He was eventually sentenced to prison and began serving his sentence in 1925. When his sentence was commuted two years later, Garvey was deported to Jamaica. With his imprisonment and deportation, his organization in the United States lost much of its momentum. Garvey spent the last years of his life in London and died in 1940.

....

Marcus saw what many Africans never see till date, he believed economic independence of Africa will bring about a true political independent. He also realizes that self-worth and religious independence are pre-requisite to free the mind of the people. He knows that production is what drives national economy. Garvey showed the right way.

He touted capitalism as the tool that would establish African Americans as an independent group. Garvey believed economic success was the quickest and most effective way to independence which is the truth.

"Until you produce what the white man has produced," he claimed, "you will not be his equal."

In 1919 he established the Negro Factories Corporation and offered stock for African Americans to buy. He wanted to produce everything that a nation needed so that African Americans could completely rely on their own efforts. At one point the corporation operated three grocery stores, two restaurants, a printing plant, a steam laundry, and owned several buildings and trucks in New York City alone. His most famous economic venture was a shipping company known as the Black Star Line.

"Our success educationally, industrially, politically is based upon the protection of a nation founded by ourselves and that nation can be nowhere else but in Africa".

The present African countries are contraption created by the Europeans. Africa has the right to create their country based on the wish and aspiration of the people.

To promote unity, Garvey encouraged African Americans to be concerned with themselves first. He stated after World War One that "the first dying that is to be done by the black man in the future will be done to make himself free. And then when we are finished, if we have any charity to bestow, we may die for the white man. But as for me, I think I have stopped dying for him." Black people had to do the work that success and independence demanded, and, most importantly, they had to do that work for themselves.

"If you want liberty," claimed Garvey to a meeting held in 1921, "you yourselves must strike the blow. If you must be free, you must become so through your own effort."

This was exactly what David, Moses and Elijah did, they protected their people only. They were called men of God in the bible. This is true biblical love. Even God himself wage countless war for the Israelites only.

Garvey claimed that African Americans should view God "through our own spectacles." If whites could view God as white, then blacks could view God as black. In 1924 the convention canonized Jesus Christ as a "Black Man of Sorrows" and the Virgin Mary as a "Black Madonna." Garvey used that image as an inspiration to succeed in this life, for African Americans needed to worship a God that understood their plight, understood their suffering, and would help them overcome their present state. Garvey was not interested in promoting hope in the afterlife. Success in this life was the key. Achieving economic, cultural, social, and political success would free African Americans in this life. The afterlife would take care of itself.

True independence goes beyond electing a black president, it is about worshiping a black God, wearing a black made shirt, driving made in Africa car, using a refined in Africa fuel, prosecute other world leaders in establish and control by Africa court. These were what Garvey advocated; true independence. This is the true semblance of God.

After surveying the racial situation in America, Garvey was convinced that integration would never happen and that only economic, political, and cultural success on the part of African Americans would bring about equality and respect.

Today blacks are still discriminated all over the world. In America, the police are killing the blacks, in Israel black Jews are discriminated. Garvey was able to see the future and proffer a solution. This is an all knowing character. Segregation will have been solved by segregation, black need to pursue economic power, own their cinema, create their public transport, build their restaurant etc, and stop whites from using these in America, by now segregation will have been a thing of the past. "Liberate the minds of men and ultimately you will liberate the body of men"

Providence is defined in oxford learners dictionary as the way in which God or nature cares for and protect all creature.

How exactly God or nature does cares for all creatures?

It is through her natural laws, and one of such law just as photosynthesis is what Garvey stated above. Garvey provided divine direction to his people at several occasion, he was provident, a quality possessed by a true man of God.

By 1922 his rhetoric shifted away from a confrontational stance against white America to a position of separatism mixed with just enough cooperation. He applauded whites who promoted the idea of sending African Americans back to Africa.

Garvey decided not to sugar coat the truth rather went raw and uncensored. He pointed out that we must worship a God that looks like us; that we should go for economic power and further segregates from the white; he said that we should create our nation in Africa and produce by ourselves and for ourselves everything we need. These were raw truth which only a true man of God will say.

Garvey led the vision of true independence; he propagated economic, cultural, political, religious and technological independence of Africa. Like Moses, David, Shemaih, he led a vision that will add true value to the life of his people.

Our churches today and their men of God led a vision of higher membership, promise of heaven, multiplication of branches and similar vision. Such visions add no real value to the life of the followers.

Garvey knew African Americans would not take action if they did not change their perceptions. He hammered home the idea of racial pride by celebrating the African past and encouraging African Americans to be proud of their heritage and proud of the way they looked. Garvey proclaimed "black is beautiful" long before it became popular in the 1960s. He wanted African Americans to see themselves as members of a mighty race. "We must calonize our own saints, create our own martyrs, and elevate to positions of fame, honor black men and women who have made their distinct contributions to our racial history." He encouraged parents to give their children "dolls that look like them to play with and cuddle," he did not want black people think of themselves in a defeated way. "I am the equal of any white man; I want you to feel the same way."

Garvey organized his group in a way that made those sentiments visible. He created an African Legion that dressed in military garb, uniformed matching bands, and other auxiliary groups such as the Black Cross Nurses.

Kwame Nkrumah

"The best way of learning to be an independent sovereign state is to be an independent sovereign state" Kwame Nkrumah Kwame I am happy to be here in Addis Ababa on this most historic occasion. I bring with me the hopes and fraternal greetings of the government and people of Ghana. Our objective is African union now. There is no time to waste. We must unite now or perish. I am confident that by our concerted effort and determination, we shall lay here the foundations for a continental Union of African States. A whole continent has imposed a mandate upon us to lay the foundation of our union at this conference. It is our responsibility to execute this mandate by creating here and now, the formula upon which the requisite superstructure may be created.

On this continent, it has not taken us long to discover that the struggle against colonialism does not end with the attainment of national independence. Independence is only the prelude to a new and more involved struggle for the right to conduct our own economic and social affairs; to construct our society according to our aspirations, unhampered by crushing and humiliating neo-colonialist controls and interference.

From the start we have been threatened with frustration where rapid change is imperative and with instability where sustained effort and ordered rule are indispensable. No sporadic act or pious resolution can resolve our present problems. Nothing will be of avail, except the united act of a united Africa. We have already reached the stage where we must unite or sink into that condition which has made Latin America the unwilling and distressed prey of imperialism after one-and-a-half centuries of political independence.

As a continent, we have emerged into independence in a different age, with imperialism grown stronger, more ruthless and experienced, and more dangerous in its international associations. Our economic advancement demands the end of colonialist and neo-colonialist domination of Africa. But just as we understood that the shaping of our national destinies required each of our political independence and bent all our strength to this attainment, so we must recognize that our economic independence resides in our African union and requires the same concentration upon the political achievement. The unity of our continent, no less than our separate independence, will be delayed if, indeed, we do not lose it, by hobnobbing with colonialism.

African unity is, above all, a political kingdom which can only be gained by political means. The social and economic development of Africa will come only within the political kingdom, not the other way round. Is it not unity alone that can weld us into an effective force, capable of creating our own progress and making our valuable contribution to world peace? Which independent African state, which of you here will claim that its financial structure and banking institutions are fully harnessed to its national development?

Which will claim that its material resources and human energies are available for its own national aspirations? Which will disclaim a substantial measure of disappointment and disillusionment in its agricultural and urban development? In independent Africa, we are already re-experiencing the instability and frustration which existed under colonial rule. We are fast learning that political independence is not enough to rid us of the consequences of colonial rule. The movement of the masses of the people of Africa for freedom from that kind of rule was not only a revolt against the conditions which it imposed. Our people supported us in our fight for independence because they believed that African governments could cure the ills of the past in a way which could never be accomplished under colonial rule.

If, therefore, now that we are independent we allow the same conditions to exist that existed in colonial days, all the resentment which overthrew colonialism will be mobilized against us. The resources are there. It is for us to marshal them in the active service of our people. Unless we do this by our concerted efforts, within the framework of our combined planning, we shall not progress at the tempo demanded by today's events and the mood of our people. The symptoms of our troubles will grow, and the troubles themselves become chronic. It will then be too late for pan-African unity to secure for us stability and tranquillity in our labours for a continent of social justice and material well-being.

Our continent certainly exceeds all the others in potential hydroelectric power, which some experts assess as 42% of the world's total. What need is there for us to remain hewers of wood and drawers of water for the industrialized areas of the world? It is said, of course, that we have no capital, no industrial skill, no communications, and no internal markets, and that we cannot even agree among ourselves how best to utilize our resources for our own social needs. Yet all stock exchanges in the world are preoccupied with Africa's gold, diamonds, uranium, platinum, copper and iron ore.

Our capital flows out in streams to irrigate the whole system of Western economy. Fifty-two per cent of the gold in Fort Knox at this moment, where the USA stores its bullion, is believed to have originated from our shores. Africa provides more than 60% of the world's gold. A great deal of the uranium for nuclear power, of copper for electronics, titanium for supersonic projectiles, iron and steel for heavy industries, other minerals and raw materials for lighter industries —the basic economic might of the foreign powers —come from our continent. Experts have estimated that the Congo Basin alone can produce enough food crops to satisfy the requirements of nearly half the population of the whole world, and here we sit talking about gradualism, talking about step by step. Are you afraid to tackle the bull by the horn? For centuries, Africa has been the milk cow of the Western world. Was it not our continent that helped the Western world to build up its accumulated wealth?

We have the resources. It was colonialism in the first place that prevented us from accumulating the effective capital; but we ourselves have failed to make full use of our power in independence to mobilize our resources for the most effective take-off into thorough-going economic and social development.

We have been too busy nursing our separate states to understand fully the basic need of our union, rooted in common purpose, common planning and common endeavor. A union that ignores these fundamental necessities will be but a sham. It is only by uniting our productive capacity and the resultant production that we can amass capital. And once we start, the momentum will increase. With capital controlled by our own banks, harnessed to our own true industrial and agricultural development, we shall make our advance.

We shall accumulate machinery and establish steel works, iron foundries and factories; we shall link the various states of our continent with communications by land, sea, and air. We shall cable from one place to another, phone from one place to the other and astound the world with our hydro-electric power; we shall drain marshes and swamps, clear infested areas, feed the undernourished, and rid our people of parasites and disease. Camels and donkeys no more

It is within the possibility of science and technology to make even the Sahara bloom into a vast field with verdant vegetation for agricultural and industrial development. We shall harness the radio, television, giant printing presses to lift our people from the dark recesses of illiteracy. A decade ago, these would have been visionary words, the fantasies of an idle dreamer. But this is the age in which science has transcended the limits of the material world, and technology has invaded the silence of nature.

Time and space have been reduced to unimportant abstractions. Giant machines make roads, clear forests, dig dams, lay out aerodromes; monster trucks and planes distribute goods; huge laboratories manufacture drugs; complicated geological surveys are made; mighty power stations are built; colossal factories erected —all at an incredible speed. The world is no longer moving through bush paths or on camels and donkeys.

We cannot afford to pace our needs, our development, our security, to the gait of camels and donkeys. We cannot afford not to cut down the overgrown bush of outmoded attitudes that obstruct our path to the modern open road of the widest and earliest achievement of economic independence and the raising up of the lives of our people to the highest level.

Even for other continents lacking the resources of Africa, this is the age that sees the end of human want. For us it is a simple matter of grasping with certainty our heritage by using the political might of unity. All we need to do is to develop with our united strength the enormous resources of our continent.

What use to the farmer is education and mechanization, what use is even capital for development, unless we can ensure for him a fair price and a ready market? What has the peasant, worker and farmer gained from political independence, unless we can ensure for him a fair return for his labour and a higher standard of living? Unless we can establish great industrial complexes in Africa, what have the urban worker, and those peasants on overcrowded land gained from political independence? If they are to remain unemployed or in unskilled occupation, what will avail them the better facilities for education, technical training, energy, and ambition which independence enables us to provide?

There is hardly any African state without a frontier problem with its adjacent neighbours. It would be futile for me to enumerate them because they are already so familiar to us all. But let me suggest that this fatal relic of colonialism will drive us to war against one another as our unplanned and uncoordinated industrial development expands, just as what happened in Europe. Unless we succeed in arresting the danger through mutual understanding on fundamental issues and through African unity, which will render existing boundaries obsolete and superfluous, we shall fought in vain for independence.

Only African unity can heal this festering sore of boundary disputes between our various states. The remedy for these ills is ready in our hands. It stares us in the face at every customs barrier, it shouts on us from every African heart. By creating a true political union of all the independent states of Africa, with executive powers for political direction, we can tackle hopefully every emergency and every complexity.

This is because we have emerged in the age of science and technology in which poverty, ignorance, and disease are no longer the masters, but the retreating foes of mankind. Above all, we have emerged at a time when a continental land mass like Africa with its population approaching 300 million is necessary to the economic capitalization and profitability of modern productive methods and techniques. No one of us working singly and individually can successfully attain the fullest development.

Certainly, in this circumstances, it will not be possible to give adequate assistance to sister states trying, against the most difficult conditions, to improve their economic and social structures. Only a united Africa functioning under a union government can forcefully mobilize the material and moral resources of our separate countries and apply them efficiently and energetically to bring a rapid change in the conditions of our people.

United we must. Without necessarily sacrificing our sovereignties, big or small, we can here and now forge a political union based on defence, foreign affairs and diplomacy, and a common citizenship, an African currency, an African monetary zone, and an African central bank. We must unite in order to achieve the full liberation of our continent. We need a common defence system with African high command to ensure the stability and security of Africa. We have been charged with this sacred task by our own people, and we cannot betray their trust by failing them. We will be mocking the hopes of our people if we show the slightest hesitation or delay in tackling realistically this question of African unity.

We need unified economic planning for Africa. Until the economic power of Africa is in our hands, the masses can have no real concern and no real interest for safeguarding our security, for ensuring the stability of our regimes, and for bending their strength to the fulfillment of our ends. With our united resources, energies and talents we have the means, as soon as we show the will, to transform the economic structures of our individual states from poverty to wealth, from inequality to the satisfaction of popular needs. Only on a continental basis shall we be able to plan the proper utilization of all our resources for the full development of our continent.

How else will we retain our own capital for own development?

How else will we establish an internal market for our own industries? By belonging to different economic zones, how will we break down the currency and trading barriers between African states, and how will the economically stronger states be able to assist the weaker and less developed states?

It is important to remember that independent financing and independent development cannot take place without an independent currency. A currency system that is backed by the resources of a foreign state is ipso facto subject to the trade and financial arrangements of that foreign country.

Because we have so many customs and currency barriers as a result of being subject to the different currency systems of foreign powers, this has served to widen the gap between us in Africa. How, for example, can related communities and families trade with, and support one another successfully, if they find themselves divided by national boundaries and currency restrictions? The only alternative open to them in these circumstances is to use smuggled currency and enrich national and international racketeers and crooks who prey upon our financial and economic difficulties, our resources.

No independent African state today by itself has a chance to follow an independent course of economic development, and many of us who have tried to do this have been almost ruined or have had to return to the fold of the former colonial rulers. This position will not change unless we have a unified policy working at the continental level. The first step towards our cohesive economy would be a unified monetary zone, with, initially, an agreed common parity for our currencies. To facilitate this arrangement, Ghana would change to a decimal system.

When we find that the arrangement of a fixed common parity is working successfully, there would seem to be no reason for not instituting one common currency and a single bank of issue. With a common currency from one common bank of issue, we should be able to stand erect on our own feet because such an arrangement would be fully backed by the combined national products of the states composing the union. After all, the purchasing power of money depends on productivity and the productive exploitation of the natural, human and physical resources of the nation. While we are assuring our stability by a common defence system, and our economy is being orientated beyond foreign control by a common currency, monetary zone, and central bank of issue, we can investigate the resources of our continent. We can begin to ascertain whether in reality we are the richest, and not, as we have been taught to believe, the poorest among the continents. We can determine whether we possess the largest potential in hydro-electric power, and whether we can harness it and other sources of energy to our industries. We can proceed to plan our industrialization on a continental scale, and to build up a common market for nearly 300 million people. Common continental planning for the industrial and agricultural development of Africa is a vital necessity!

So many blessings flow from our unity; so many disasters must follow on our continued disunity. The hour of history which has brought us to this assembly is a revolutionary hour. It is the hour of decision. The masses of the people of Africa are crying for unity. The people of Africa call for breaking down of the boundaries that keep them apart. They demand an end to the border disputes between sister African states —disputes that arise out of the artificial barriers raised by colonialism. It was colonialism's purpose that divided us. It was colonialism's purpose that left us with our border irredentism that rejected our ethnic and cultural fusion.

Our people call for unity so that they may not lose their patrimony in the perpetual service of neo-colonialism. In their fervent push for unity, they understand that only its realization will give full meaning to their freedom and our African independence.

It is this popular determination that must move us on to a union of independent African states. In delay lies danger to our well-being, to our very existence as free states.

It has been suggested that our approach to unity should be gradual, that it should go piecemeal. This point of view conceives of Africa as a static entity with "frozen" problems which can be eliminated one by one and when all have been cleared then we can come together and say: "Now all is well, let us now unite."

This view takes no account of the impact of external pressures. Nor does it take cognisance of the danger that delay can deepen our isolations and exclusiveness; that it can enlarge our differences and set us drifting further and further apart into the net of neo-colonialism, so that our union will become nothing but a fading hope, and the great design of Africa's full redemption will be lost, perhaps, forever.

The dangers of regionalism

The view is also expressed that our difficulties can be resolved simply by a greater collaboration through cooperative association in our inter-territorial relationships. This way of looking at our problems denies a proper conception of their inter-relationship and mutuality. It denies faith in a future for African advancement in African independence. It betrays a sense of solution only in continued reliance upon external sources through bilateral agreements for economic and other forms of aid.

The fact is that although we have been cooperating and associating with one another in various fields of common endeavour even before colonial times, this has not given us the continental identity and the political and economic force which would help us to deal effectively with the complicated problems confronting us in Africa today.

As far as foreign aid is concerned, a United Africa should be in a more favourable position to attract assistance from foreign sources. There is the far more compelling advantage which this arrangement offers, in that aid will come from anywhere to a United Africa because our bargaining power would become infinitely greater. We shall no longer be dependent upon aid from restricted sources. We shall have the world to choose from.

What are we looking for in Africa? Are we looking for Charters, conceived in the light of the United Nations' example? A type of United Nations Organization whose decisions are framed on the basis of resolutions that in our experience have sometimes been ignored by member states? Where groupings are formed and pressures develop in accordance with the interest of the groups concerned?

Or is it intended that Africa should be turned into a loose organization of states on the model of the Organization of American States, in which the weaker states within it can be at the mercy of the stronger or more powerful ones politically or economically and all at the mercy of some powerful outside nation or group of nations? Is this the kind of association we want for ourselves in the United Africa we all speak of with such feeling and emotion?

We all want a united Africa, united not only in our concept of what unity connotes, but united in our common desire to move forward together in dealing with all the problems that can best be solved only on a continental basis.

We meet here today not as Ghanaians, Guineans, Egyptians, Algerians, Moroccans, Malians, Liberians, Congolese or Nigerians, but as Africans. Africans united in our resolve to remain here until we have agreed on the basic principles of a new compact of unity among ourselves which guarantees for us and our future a new arrangement of continental government. If we succeed in establishing a new set of principles as the basis of a new charter for the establishment of a continental unity of Africa, and the creation of social and political progress for our people, then in my view, this conference should mark the end of our various groupings and regional blocs.

But if we fail and let this grand and historic opportunity slips by, then we shall give way to greater dissension and division among us for which the people of Africa will never forgive us. And the popular and progressive forces and movements within Africa will condemn us. I am sure therefore that we shall not fail them. To this end, I propose for your consideration the following: As a first step, a declaration of principles uniting and binding us together and to which we must all faithfully and loyally adhere, and laying the foundations of unity, should be set down.

As a second and urgent step for the realization of the unification of Africa, an All-Africa Committee of Foreign Ministers should be set up now. The Committee should establish on behalf of the heads of our governments, a permanent body of officials and experts to work out machinery for the union government of Africa. This body of officials and experts should be made up of two of the best brains from each independent African state. The various charters of existing groupings and other relevant documents could also be submitted to the officials and experts.

We must also decide on a location where this body of officials and experts will work as the new headquarters or capital of our union government. Some central place in Africa might be the fairest suggestion, either in Bangui in the Central African Republic or Leopoldville [Kinshasa] in Congo. My colleagues may have other proposals.

The Committee of Foreign Ministers, officials and experts, should be empowered to establish: (1) A commission to frame a constitution for a Union Government of African States. (2) A commission to work out a continent-wide plan for a unified or common economic and industrial programme for Africa; this should include proposals for setting up: a common market for Africa; an African currency; an African monetary zone; an African central bank; a continental communication system; a commission to draw up details for a common foreign policy and diplomacy; a commission to produce plans for a common system of defence; a commission to make proposals for a common African citizenship. Africa must unite!

Endnote

The day after Nkrumah's speech, the 32 independent African nations assembled in Addis Ababa failed to go the full hog for a strong United States of Africa. Instead they settled for a loose and weak Organization of African Unity (OAU) whose Charter was signed the same day (25 May 1963) by the following countries: Algeria, Burundi, Cameroon, Central African Republic, Congo (Brazzaville), Congo (Kinshasa), Dahomey, Ethiopia, Gabon, Ghana, Guinea, Côte d'Ivoire, Liberia, Libya, Malagasy, Mali, Mauritania, Morocco, Niger, Nigeria, Rwanda, Senegal, Sierra Leone, Somalia, Sudan, Tanganyika, Tshad [later Chad], Togo, Tunisia, Uganda, Egypt, and Upper Volta [later Burkina Faso].

....

Nkruma was a true man of God in all its ramifications. Let's examine him

The all-knowing ability of God was his embodiment. He knew before time that the only way to combat African problems, to cure our diseases, to achieve success individually and collectively as a people, to be totally delivered from the bondage of neo-colonialism is for Africa to unite. He proposed a union government but the lesser African leaders, the infidel couldn't see the future. A true man of God must be all knowing.

Let's not get things mixed up here, a pastor who prophesies and it comes to pass is of God but if one of his prophesy fail to be fulfilled, know that he is not of God. Nkruma prophesied that Africa is not *yet* independent until we take control of our economy and culture. Today, evidence abound that we are economically, technologically, religiously, politically and culturally enslaved.

"As a continent, we have emerged into independence in a different age, with imperialism grown stronger, more ruthless and experienced, *and more dangerous in its international associations.* Our economic advancement demands the end of colonialist and neo-colonialist domination of Africa".

I italic the sentence "more dangerous in its international association" Nkruma knew that international associations are tools to enslave Africa. Today, we are members of the united nation, international criminal court, international monetary fund, world trade organization etc. If we look critically into this association, we are always at the loose end. Only a true man of God will foresee this.

"No independent African state today by itself has a chance to follow an independent course of economic action development, and many of us who have tried to do this have been almost ruined or have to return to the fold of the former colonial rulers. This position will not change unless we have a unified policy working at the continental level. The first step towards our cohesive economy would be a unified monetary zone, with initially, an agreed common parity for our currencies. To facilitate this arrangement, Ghana would change to a decimal system"

Again, I italic the sentence *"or have to return to the fold of the former colonial rulers"* this prophesy has been fulfilled today. Only a true man of God said things which come to fulfillment. The good thing is he offered a way to avoid this catastrophe from taking place yet we refuse to adopt it.

Nkruma led a vision of African unity. What vision is your pastor leading? The unity of Africa under a union government with tribal region constituting independent state with the central government in charge of defense, trade, foreign policy while the regional state will control the police, agriculture, science and technology, infrastructure.

Nkruma led this vision which will have scuttled the present world order. The unity of Africa will bring an end to all foreign depth owned by present African countries. It will destroy all United States military bases in Africa, lead to control of African resources by Africans, control of African monetary system and foreign exchange by Africans and development of science and technology by African.

Providence is defined as foreseeing care and guidance of God and nature over the creatures of the earth or his direction of affairs of humans.

"But just as we understood that the shaping of our national destinies required of each of us our political independence and bent all our strength to this attainment, so we must recognize that our economic independence reside in our African union and require the same concentration upon the political achievement. The unity of our continent, no less than our separate independence, will be delayed if, indeed, we do not lose it, by hobnobbing with colonialism"

"Our capital flows out in streams to irrigate the whole system of western economy. Fifty-two per cent of the gold in fort knox at this moment, were the USA stores its bullion, is believed to have originated from our shores. Africa produces more than 60% of the world's gold. A great deal of uranium for nuclear power, of copper for electronics, of titanium for supersonic projectiles, of iron and steel for heavy industries, of other minerals and raw materials for lighter industries-the basic economic might of the foreign powers-come from our continent"

Nkruma directed the affairs of Africa toward sustainable development and true independence. This is an act of a true man of God, this is an attribute of God, it was only God who directed the affairs of the Israelite toward true independent from Egypt and the Canaanites.

Veracity means truth telling

"On this continent, it has not taking us long to discover that the struggle against colonialism does not end with the attainment of national independence. Independence is only the prelude to a new and more involved struggle for the right to conduct our own economic and social affairs: to construct our society according to our aspirations, unhampered by the crushing and humiliating neo-colonialist controls and interference"

Today we all know that the imperial power attempted to push gay into our continent, today we know that the united states of America have military base all over Africa, AFRICOM is for the control of Africa, today the colonial and imperial powers still overthrow government in Africa. Today, foreign companies handle construction and drilling of our resources, they control our economy.

Nkrumah tells us this raw truth before it happens just as Elijah predicted the fall of kingdoms before Israelite went for war. This can only be done by a true man of God.

"But if we fail and let this grand and historic opportunity slips by, then we shall give way to greater dissension and division among us for which the people of Africa will never forgive us. And the popular and progressive forces and movements within Africa will condemn us. I am sure therefore that we shall not fail them. To this end, I propose for your consideration the following: As a first step, a declaration of principles uniting and binding us together and to which we must all faithfully and loyally adhere, and laying the foundations of unity, should be set down.

As a second and urgent step for the realization of the unification of Africa, an All-Africa Committee of Foreign Ministers should be set up now. The Committee should establish on behalf of the heads of our governments, a permanent body of officials and experts to work out machinery for the union government of Africa. This body of officials and experts should be made up of two of the best brains from each independent African state. The various charters of existing groupings and other relevant documents could also be submitted to the officials and experts.

We must also decide on a location where this body of officials and experts will work as the new headquarters or capital of our union government. Some central place in Africa might be the fairest suggestion, either in Bangui in the Central African Republic or Leopoldville [Kinshasa] in Congo. My colleagues may have other proposals.

The Committee of Foreign Ministers, officials and experts, should be empowered to establish: (1) A commission to frame a constitution for a Union Government of African States. (2) A commission to work out a continent-wide plan for a unified or common economic and industrial programme for Africa; this should include proposals for setting up: a common market for Africa; an African currency; an African monetary zone; an African central bank; a continental communication system; a commission to draw up details for a common foreign policy and diplomacy; a commission to produce plans for a common system of defence; a commission to make proposals for a common African citizenship. Africa must unite!"

Which pastor ever contributed sound and useful idea for the development of the society? Churches today don't care about the society they operate, all what matter to them is expansion and membership. How can you live in a society without caring about the society as a man of God?

Elijah cared about his society that was why he challenged the prophet of Baal in an open contest. Moses cared about his people, that was why he killed the Egyptian who fought with a Jew. Nkrumah cared for his people, that was why he fought for the political independence of Ghana and eventually, economic independence of Africa. Your pastor cares for you that is why he demanded for tithe and offering every Sunday and promise of reward from heaven. Think.

These men were thought leaders, initiators while your pastors are copycats and profit mongers.

Nkruma understood that unity is power, in Nigeria APC, an opposition party just won the presidential election after sixteen years ruled by PDP. They defeated a seating president because they unite four parties to form a strong opposition.

Nkruma proposed this unity which can alleviate Africa from poverty and gave her a strong base to resist imperial influence and control but we refused it, hence we lose. We all know that unity is power, Nkrumah showed us the way to unity, he showed the right way, an attribute of a true man of God.

Leading you to heaven is what your pastor claimed to be doing while he is building his own paradise here on earth. Nkruma instructed us on how to build an African paradise. Tell me, who is a true man of God, your pastor or Nkruma?

Thomas Sankara
By Désiré-Joseph Katihabwa
Sunday, 3 May 2009

Captain[6]Thomas Isidore Noël Sankara (December 21, 1949 – October 15, 1987) was the leader of Burkina Faso (formerly known as Upper Volta) from 1983 to 1987. While noted for his personal charisma and praised for promoting health and women's rights, he also antagonised many vested interests in the country. He was overthrown and assassinated in a coup d'état led by Blaise Compaoré on October 15, 1987, sometimes believed to have been at the instruction of France.

Thomas Sankara was the son of Marguerite Sankara (died March 6, 2000) and Sambo Joseph Sankara (1919 – August 4, 2006), a gendarme. Born into a Roman Catholic family, "Thom'Sank" was a Silmi-Mossi, an ethnic group that originated with marriage between Mossi men and women of the pastoralist Fulani people. The Silmi-Mossi are among the least advantaged in the Mossi caste system. He attended primary school in Gaoua and high school in Bobo-Dioulasso, the country's second city.

His father fought in the French army during World War II and was detained by the Nazis. Sankara's family wanted him to become a Catholic priest. According to some sources, he never lost his Catholic faith despite his Marxist tendencies. Fittingly for a country with a large Muslim population, he was also familiar with the Qur'an.

Military career

After basic military training in secondary school in 1966, Sankara began his military career at the age of 19, and a year later he was sent to Madagascar for officers training at Antsirabe where he witnessed popular uprising in 1971 and 1972. Returning to Upper Volta in 1972, in 1974 he fought in a border war between Upper Volta and Mali.

He became a popular figure in the capital of Ouagadougou. The fact that he was a decent guitarist (he played in a band named "Tout-à-Coup Jazz") and liked motorbikes may have contributed to his charisma.

In 1976 he became commander of the Commando Training Centre in Pô. In the same year he met Blaise Compaoré in Morocco. During the presidency of Colonel Saye Zerbo, a group of young officers formed a secret organisation "Communist Officers' Group" (Regroupement des officiers communistes, or ROC) the best-known members being Henri Zongo, Jean-Baptiste, Boukary Lingani, Compaoré and Sankara.

Government posts

Sankara was appointed Secretary of State for Information in the military government in September 1981, journying to his first cabinet meeting on a bicycle, but he resigned on April 21, 1982 in opposition to what he saw as the regime's anti-labour drift, declaring "Misfortune to those who gag the people!" ("Malheur à ceux qui baillonnent le peuple!")

After another coup (November 7, 1982) brought to power Major-Doctor Jean-Baptiste Ouédraogo, Sankara became prime minister in January 1983, but he was dismissed (May 17) and placed under house arrest after a visit by the French president's son and African affairs adviser Jean-Christophe Mitterrand. Henri Zongo and Jean-Baptiste Boukary Lingani were also placed under arrest; this caused a popular uprising.

President

A coup d'état organised by Blaise Compaoré made Sankara President on August 4, 1983 at the age of 33. The coup d'état was supported by Libya which was, at that time, on the verge of war with France in Chad.

Sankara saw himself as a revolutionary and was inspired by the examples of Cuba and Ghana's military leader, Flight Lt. Jerry Rawlings. As President, he promoted the "Democratic and Popular Revolution" (Révolution démocratique et populaire, or RDP).

The ideology of the Revolution was defined by Sankara as anti-imperialist in a speech of October 2, 1983, the Discours d'orientation politique (DOP), written by his close associate Valère Somé. His policy was oriented toward fighting corruption, promoting reforestation, averting famine, and making education and health real priorities.

Abolition of chiefs' privileges

The government suppressed many of the powers held by tribal chiefs such as their right to receive tribute payment and obligatory labour. The CDRs (Comités de Défense de la Révolution) were formed as popular mass organizations and armed. In some areas they deteriorated into gangs of armed thugs. Sankara's government also initiated a form of military conscription with the SERNAPO (Service National et Populaire). Both were a counterweight to the power of the army.

In 1984, on the first anniversary of his accession, he renamed the country Burkina Faso, meaning "the land of upright people" in Mossi and Djula, the two major languages of the country. He also gave it a new flag and wrote a new national anthem.

Women's rights

Sankara's government included a large number of women. Improving women's status was one of Sankara's explicit goals, an unprecedented policy priority in West Africa. His government banned female genital's cutting, condemned polygamy, and promoted contraception. The Burkinabé government was also the first African government to publicly recognize AIDS as a major threat to Africa.

Sankara had some original initiatives that contributed to his popularity and brought some international media attention to the Burkinabé revolution:

*   He sold most of the government fleet of Mercedes cars and made the Renault 5 (the cheapest car sold in Burkina Faso at that time) the official service car of the ministers;

* He formed an all-women motorcycle personal guard.
* In Ouagadougou, Sankara converted the army's provision store into a state-owned supermarket open to everyone (the first supermarket in the country).

Second Agacher strip war

In 1985 Burkina Faso organised a general population census. During the census some Fula camps in Mali were visited by mistake by Burkinabé census agents. The Malian government claimed that it was an act of sovereignty on the Agacher strip and on Christmas Day 1985, tensions with Mali erupted in a war that lasted five days and killed about 100 people (most victims were civilians killed by a bomb dropped on the market place in Ouahigouya by a Malian MiG plane). The conflict is known as the "Christmas war" in Burkina Faso.

Assassination

On October 15, 1987 Sankara was killed with twelve other officials in a coup d'état organised by his former colleague, Compaoré. Deterioration in relations with neighbouring countries was one of the reasons given by Compaoré for his action. Prince Johnson, a former Liberian warlord allied to Charles Taylor, told Liberia's Truth and Reconciliation Commission (TRC) that it was engineered by Charles Taylor. After the coup, Sankara was known to be dead, some CDRs mounted an armed resistance to the army for several days.

Sankara was quickly buried in an unmarked grave. A week prior to his death Sankara addressed people and said that "while revolutionaries as individuals can be murdered, you cannot kill ideas."

Indeed, Africa and the world are yet to recover from Sankara's assassination. Just as we have yet to recover from the loss of Patrice Lumumba, Kwame Nkrumah, Eduardo Mondlane, Amilcar Cabral, Steve Biko, Samora Machel, Muamar Gadhafi and John Garang, to name only a few, names many Africans never heard about because our educational system is not designed to be truly African.

While malevolent forces have not used the same methods to eliminate each of these great men of God, they have been guided by the same motive: to keep Africa in chains. We need another savior. The first set of African leaders who really feel and understand colonialism were eliminated. Between 1961 and 1973, six African independence leaders were assassinated. They killed our prophet just as they killed Jesus Christ.

[7]**Hear Thomas Sankara in his own words:**

"If you take a walk around Ouagadougou and make a list of the mansions you see, you will note that they belong to just a minority. How many of you who have been assigned to Ouagadougou from the farthest corners of the country have had to move every night because you've been thrown out of the house you have rented? To those who have acquired houses and land through corruption we say: start to tremble. If you have stolen, tremble, because we will come after you". March 26, 1983

"The basic purpose and main objective of the National Council of the Revolution is to defend the interest of the Voltaic people and fulfill their aspirations toward liberty, genuine independence, economic and social progress". August 4, 1983

"To state it clearl, we buy more from abroad than we sell. An economy that functions on such a basis is headed for increasing ruin and catastrophe" October 2, 1983. I love this.

"Aid to Burkina Faso must serve to strengthen not undermine, our sovereignty. It should help to destroy the need for further aid. All aid that puts further aid to death is welcome in Burkina Faso. But all aid that creates a beggar mentality, we will have to do without".

August 1984

"We propose that the structures of the UN be changed to put an end to the scandal surrounding the right to veto" October 4, 1984

"The greatest difficulty we have faced is the neocolonial spirit that exists in this country. We were colonized by a country, France that left us with certain habits. For us, being successful in life, being happy, meant trying to live as they do in France, like the richest people of Frence." March 17, 1985.

"We have to work at decolonizing our mentality and achieving happiness within the limits of sacrifice we should be willing to make. We have to recondition our people to accept themselves as they are, not to be ashamed of their real situation, to be satisfied with it, to glory in it." 1985.

This was a clarion call for mental revolution by Thomas Sankara.

"A party has to have structures, leadership and representatives. Who would do this other than those who are there already and who are not necessarily the most combative? All kinds of people would swear by this party in order to be sure of a post, a little bit the way the carving up of government ministries is viewed." 1985

"We must even put a stop to certain kinds of praise that are poorly disguised and badly controlled expressions of feudal reflexes. This song, for example "oh, Thomas Sankara may he forever be President" is not good".

April 4, 1986

"We are actors in the international arena, and we have the right to choose a political and economic system true to our aspirations. We have the right to fight for a more just and more peaceful world, regardless of the fact that we have neither large industrial cartels nor nuclear weapons". August 27, 1987.

We can equally sanction any country that go contrary to our rule.

"It is always at the side of a woman that we become men again, and every man is a child for every woman." March 8, 1987

"I have told myself, either I'll finish up an old man somewhere in a library reading books, or I'll meet with a violent end, since we have so many enemies. Once you've accepted that reality, it's just a question of time. It will happen today or tomorrow."

October 8th, 1987

One week after Thomas Sankara made this last remark, he was murdered but like Don Rojas observation "Thomas Sankara's murder cannot erase the valuable contributions in both theory and practice he has made to the world's revolutionary process."

Homeland or death, we will triumph!

Thomas Sankara was a true embodiment of God. He exhibited the following attribute;

Sankara stood for one thing; the eradication of imperial influence in his country. He refuses loan from IMF because he knew the loans were designed to further enslave his people. He increased the literacy of his people and gave rights to women. He led a vision of a true independent state. He wanted his country to be economically, politically and culturally independent.

A truly independent state depends mostly on itself; they don't seek for aid or beg for unnecessary assistance, they love their culture. Sankara stood for this; he was an embodiment of God to his people, a true man of God.

He displayed undiluted love for the women's folk and to his people. He was the first to vaccinate his people and reduced mortality rate. Literacy level increased tremendously within two years.

Majority of our present pastors and so called men of God never pay hospital bills for their members; I said, I bet on this.

You may say Sankara treated them with government or public money, the church money is equally public money, an incorporated trustee is a public enterprise, churches are incorporated trustees. So the responsibility to treat and take care of the members, the sheep lies on the pastors, the shepherd. Anything other than that depicts false doctrine.

He refused loan from IMF knowing very well that it will affect generation to come after him, this is true love, an act of a true man of God.

"To state it clearl, we buy more from abroad than we sell. An economy that functions on such a basis is headed for increasing ruin and catastrophe" October 2, 1983

"We propose that the structures of the UN be changed to put an end to the scandal surrounding the right to veto" October 4, 1984

Tell me, is there anything more righteous than the above two quotes?

We all know that productivity is the engine that drive economic growth, a country that produce technology produces wealth and a country that consume technology produces poverty. Sankara showed us the right way which ironically many African refuse to follow.

Gold found in Ghana is refined in Europe and America, crude oil found in Nigeria is drilled and refined by Europeans and Americans yet our supposed men of God are busy preaching divine prosperity when our wealth are taking away.

Do you know the united nation charter? No African nation is a permanent member of the Security Council of the united nation organization.

"The greatest difficulty we faced is the neocolonial spirit that exists in this country. We were colonized by a country, France that left us with certain habits. For us, being successful in life, being happy, meant trying to live as they do in France, like the rich people of the Frence." Marcy 17, 1985.

"We have to work at decolonizing our mentality and achieving happiness within the limits of sacrifice we should be willing to make. We have to recondition our people to accept themselves as they are, not to be ashamed of their real situation, to be satisfied with it, to glory in it" 1985

Mental slavery is a big problem in Africa today. Our culture and language are now inferior, our skin color is now a mark of shame, our local names are currently replace by foreign names. We as a people have lost our sense of uniqueness and originality. Sankara told us this truth long before now.

The Jews never forget their home land even when the land was too small for them, they never change their religion for thousands of years even when Jesus Christ attempted it. Today Judaism remains the major religion in Israel yet we abandoned our religion.

Truth is always bitter and needed to be sugar-coated for easy swallowing, Sankara presented it raw. Moses presented it raw when he told pharaoh let the people go so that they can worship their God in wilderness.

Sankara was all knowing. He knew that loans are designed to imprison the people. He knew that imperialism and neo-colonization still exist in the mind of his people and in the country. He knew that Africans felt inferior so they adopt the culture and lifestyle of their colonial masters, relegating their culture to the background. He knew that we buy more than we produce and such economy is heading to catastrophe.

Sankara watched and understood the intrigue of international politics, he questioned the veto issue of the United Nation knowing very well that such power will always be used against African people. Today we all know that the united states invade any country without recourse to the UN charter.

Today we all know that Burkina Faso's economy is ruined. Today we all know that the imperial powers still control our economy; they own the multinational companies. These were prophesies of Sankara and they have come to fulfillment. This can only be known by an all knowing God or his true embodiment, the true man of God.

Providence means prudent care and management of resources, the manifestation of divine care.

Before Sankara, Burkina Faso had an illiteracy rate of over 90%, the world's highest infant mortality rate (280 deaths for every 1,000 births), inadequate infrastructure to provide basic social services, one doctor per 50,000 people, and an average yearly income of $150 per person.

A year after Sankara took office, Burkina Faso became the first country in Africa to run mass measles vaccination campaigns. That year, with the aid of Cuban volunteers, 2.5 million children were immunized for several infectious diseases and even children from neighboring countries were vaccinated.

The alarming infant mortality rates dropped to 145 deaths per 1,000 in less than two years. In an effort to slow the advance of the Sahara Desert, Sankara launched a reforestation program that planted 10 million trees in its first year. Even today, trees are planted to celebrate birthdays, weddings and graduations. School attendance rose from 12% to 22% in just two years and was complemented by policies to encourage attendance and eventual graduation.

A campaign for the restoration of women's dignity and recognition of their role in society was launched in order to free women from the yoke of patriarchal domination. During Sankara's presidency, Burkina Faso was a leader in employing women in government posts. In a symbolic attempt to demonstrate to men what the daily realities of women's lives were like, he declared a day of solidarity with housewives and forced men to go to market and take responsibility for household duties.

Sankara refused to use the air conditioning in his office on the grounds that such luxuries were only available to a few Burkinabes.

He refused to allow his portrait to be displayed all over the country in order to prevent a cult of personality developing around him.

Shortly after coming to power he sold the government's fleet of Mercedes-Benz and purchased the far more affordable and easy to maintain Renault 5. Sankara's pragmatism and commitment to fiscal responsibility is still remembered: in 2003 critics of the Kenyan government's purchase of 12 million dollars in luxury cars advised the government to follow the example set by Sankara.

This is contrary to our so called men of God who go on private jet while their members wallow in abject poverty. Wake up brothers and sisters and embrace the true men of God, the true teaching of self-reliance; a total freedom as a person and as a people.

Freedom from religion, freedom from foreign culture, freedom from economic and technological dependence, and freedom from imperial power are the true teaching endorse by God. This was what David, Moses and Elijah taught. They were true men of God.

Odumegwu Ojukwu

[8] Nigerian-born military leader Chukwuemeka Odumegwu Ojukwu (born 1933) headed the unsuccessful move by Biafra to secede from Nigeria.

Oxford-educated Chukwuemeka Odumegwu Ojukwu joined the Nigerian army, against his wealthy father's wish, hoping to play an integral role in the nation's affairs once Nigeria had gained independence from Britain. Instead, due to his ethnic loyalties and to political events, he became the leader of the Biafrans during a bloody civil war in Nigeria. Although claiming some early victories, his forces were fighting against troops backed by Britain, Russia, and most of Europe. For three years, Odumegwu Ojukwu fought to keep Biafra from being annihilated. With supply lines cut, an estimated eight million Biafrans slowly starved to death. After the civil war ended in 1970, Odumegwu Ojukwu lived in voluntary exile. He was invited back to Nigeria in 1982, and Nigerian leaders have sought his counsel as the African nation charts its future.

Privileged Child

Chukwuemeka Odumegwu Ojukwu was born in 1933 in Zungeru, a community in the northern part of Nigeria, which was then a colony of Britain. He was the son of Sir Louis Philippe Odumegwu Ojukwu, one of the most successful businessmen among the Ibos, the largest ethnic group in Nigeria. Consequently, the younger Odumegwu Ojukwu received the best education money could buy. His primary education was at a private Catholic school in the Nigerian city of Lagos. Before he was ten years old, he was enrolled at nearby King's College as the youngest pupil in the institution's history. Two years later, Odumegwu Ojukwu's father transferred him to a school in Surrey, England, called Epson College, to finish his secondary studies. Odumegwu Ojukwu had a natural athletic ability. During his years in England, he honed his skills on the playing field when not attending classes, In school-sponsored sports, he served as captain of the rugby and soccer teams. He also set the All England Junior record in the discus throw.

In 1952, Odumegwu Ojukwu was admitted to Oxford University. He majored in history, graduating in 1955 with honors. As an undergraduate, Odumegwu Ojukwu continued to pursue his love of athletics while developing outside interests in drama and journalism. He served as a leader in the Oxford branch of the West African Students Union. he was known for his flashy sports cars, which he frequently drove at high speeds between Oxford and London. It was at Oxford that he met a female law student named Njideka; she eventually became his wife.

Away from the Sheltered Life.

With a degree from Oxford University and a wealthy father, Odumegwu Ojukwu was guaranteed access to the highest level of British colonial Nigeria, rather than relying on his father, however, he chose to enter the workforce. Odumegwu Ojukwu was hired by the Nigerian civil service and became the assistant district officer in the town of Udi, overseeing community development in rural areas. He later served in the same position in the towns of Aba and Umuahia. As a community development leader, he gained a reputation for his quick understanding of complex issues and was respected for his fair recommendations.

In 1957, in an attempt to distance himself from his privileged upbringing, he joined the army. His father was against this decision that he did not speak to his son for the next two and a half years. Meanwhile, the younger Odumegwu Ojukwu completed officer training in England at the Officer Cadet School at Eaton Hall and was commissioned a second lieutenant. After attending the Infantry School in Warminster, England, the Small Arms School in Hythe, England, and the Royal West African Frontier Force Training School in Teshie, Ghana, he returned to Nigeria in 1958 and was assigned to the Fifth Battalion in Kaduna.

When Nigeria gained independence from Britain in 1960, Odumegwu Ojukwu was quickly promoted; he held the rank of major by 1961. As one of his assignments, he served with the Nigerian First Brigade in the Congo as part of a United Nations peace-keeping program. Later, he attended the Joint Services Staff College in the United Kingdom as the first Nigerian officer. In 1963, Odumegwu Ojukwu, as a lieutenant colonel, became the first Nigerian quartermaster-general in the Nigerian Army. His first independent command came in 1965; he was assigned as commanding officer to the Fifth Battalion of the Nigerian Army in Kano.

Fragile Independence

The early years of Nigerian independence were difficult for the country. Political turmoil, riots, and ethnic rivalries resulted to a civil war in the latter half of the 1960s. Members of the largest ethnic group, the Ibos, were murdered in great numbers during the chaos, more than a million (some sources say over four million) survivors fled back to their homeland in eastern Nigeria. Odumegwu Ojukwu, the military governor of the region, assumed control in the mid-1960s in an attempt to strengthen the bargaining power of the Ibos. He first argued against secession from Nigeria by the Ibos, instead, urged easterners to accept a loosening ties with the rest of Nigeria. A 1968 article in Time magazine stated, "Odumegwu Ojukwu was a calm and reasoned voice pleading for a united Nigeria long after other powerful Ibos had angrily given up hope of preserving the union." Critics felt that because most of Odumegwu Ojukwu's inheritance from his father was in Lagos, he had a personal stake in keeping Nigeria together.

Odumegwu Ojukwu changed his stance, however, and sided with the separatists on the issue of safety for the Ibos. At one point, he and Nigerian army chief of staff Yakubu Gowon, also in control of the central Nigerian government, appeared to be nearing a compromise that would have allowed the Ibos a measure of autonomy while staying within the Nigerian federation. But

Gowon was unwilling to let the eastern region maintain a separate army, and Odumegwu Ojukwu was unsure of the ability of the Nigerian central government to protect the Ibos. Odumegwu Ojukwu reluctantly demanded independence for the easterners. He formally proclaimed the independent Republic of Biafra on May 30, 1967, during a reception in the regional capital of Enugu. At that time, he also hinted that the Nigerian central government had played a role in the genocide of the Ibo people. He then built up his army and expelled northerners from Biafra, telling them that, because of the flood of Ibo refugees, non-easterners should leave for their own safety.

Civil War

At the onset of conflict in 1967, Odumegwu Ojukwu received little sympathy or support from the international community. Nigeria, however, was backed by Britain, the Soviet Union, and most Western Europe. The Nigerian central government first established a naval blockade along the Biafran coast then sent troops, composed mostly of Muslims from the northern part of the country, to the east where they were met by Odumegwu Ojukwu's rebel forces. Initially, the Biafrans took control of strategic points in the midwestern region of Nigeria and the oil-rich Niger River Delta. The central government retaliated by sending in more armed forces, which escalated the conflict into a full-blown civil war. Odumegwu Ojukwu directed the overall strategy for Biafra in the war, but he left most of the tactical decisions to his brigade commanders and often sought advice from Ibo elders. He downplayed his role in the civil war, although the Nigerians frequently called the conflict "Ojukwu's war" and depicted the military leader as a power-mad Hitler who was shattering the unity of the new Nigeria. Odumegwu Ojukwu told New York Times Magazine reporter Lloyd Garrison, "Independence is not one man getting up and declaring it. Freedom without substance is meaningless."

By the end of 1967, Nigerian forces had regained control of the midwest and had cut off Biafran access to the sea. Although they had encircled the Biafrans, they were unable to penetrate the Ibo heartland. The Biafrans, however, were crowded into mangrove swamps and hardwood forests, unable to provide themselves with the materials of daily existence. Meanwhile, Soviet-built warplanes, many flown by hired Egyptians and British pilots, cut supply lines and inflicted heavy casualties during raids on Biafran urban centers.

Consequently, Biafrans were starving to death at a rate conservatively estimated to be approximately 1,000 people a day, according to Time. Other sources estimate that as many as 8,000 people a day died of starvation in the region during this time. Despite the hardship, the Ibo people continued to support the war effort. Odumegwu Ojukwu thus began waging a public-relations campaign to receive badly needed supplies from the rest of the world. He sent out press releases and photos showing starving Biafrans. He persuaded several countries, including Czechoslovakia, The Netherlands, and Belgium, to cut off weapons supplies to Nigeria. Odumegwu Ojukwu hoped for airlifts, which he considered a symbol of the world helping a besieged people. But by October 1969, realizing that he would receive little foreign support, he appealed for United Nations mediation to obtain terms for a cease fire and to begin peace negotiations.

The Nigerian central government, however, was not inclined to accept anything less than surrender and seemed to consider starvation a weapon of war that would preclude its having to send soldiers into battle. At about this time, Odumegwu Ojukwu told Time correspondent James Wilde, "What you are seeing now is the end of a long journey. It began in the far north of Nigeria and moved steadily southward as we were driven out from place to place. Now this path has become the road to the slaughterhouse here in the Ibo heartland." By the end of the year, 120, 000 Nigerian troops had divided Biafra in half. The rebel nation collapsed in January 1970.

After the civil war, under Gowon's supervision, the Nigerian central government took steps to ensure that the Ibos would be treated as fellow citizens rather than defeated enemies. Programs were developed to reintegrate the Ibos into a united Nigeria. Many Biafran military officers rejoined the central government as part of a general amnesty. Odumegwu Ojukwu, however, opted for voluntary exile and went to the Ivory Coast on the invitation of the nearby African nation's president. He justified his actions at that time by declaring, as quoted in Newsweek, "While I live, Biafra lives." Odumegwu Ojukwu was invited back to Nigeria by Shehu Shagari, the Nigerian government in 1982. Since then, the former Biafran leader has become active in the National Party of Nigeria. Although he was unsuccessful in a bid to be elected to the national senate, his advice is often sought by factions of the Nigerian and greater African community. He has encouraged the military to support Nigeria's slow transition toward democracy. In 1993, he publicly supported Nigeria's Republican Party because he thought it would be the best guarantor of eastern interests in national politics.

₉BIAFRA'S DECLARATION OF INDEPENDENCE, 1967 BY CHUKWUEMEKA ODUMEGWU OJUKWU

Fellow countrymen and women, the people of Eastern Nigeria:

Conscious of the supreme authority of Almighty God over all mankind, duty to yourselves and posterity; Aware that your lives and properties can no longer be protected by any Government outside Eastern Nigeria;

Believing that you are born free and have certain inalienable rights which can best be preserved by yourselves; Unwilling to be unfree partners in any association of a political or economical nature; Rejecting the authority of any person or persons other than the Military Government of Eastern Nigeria to make any imposition of whatever kind or nature upon you; Determined to dissolve all political and other ties between you and the former Federal Republic of Nigeria; Prepared to enter into such association, treaty or alliance with any sovereign state within the former Federal Republic of Nigeria and elsewhere on such terms and conditions as best to subserve your common good; Affirming your trust and confidence in me;

Having mandated me to proclaim on your behalf, and in your name, that Eastern Nigeria be a sovereign independent Republic,

Now, therefore, I, Lieutenant-Colonel Chukwuemeka Odumegwu Ojukwu, Military Governor of Eastern Nigeria, by virtue of the authority, and pursuant to the principles, recited above, do hereby solemnly proclaim that the territory and region known as and called Eastern Nigeria together with her continental shelf and territorial waters shall henceforth be an independent sovereign state of the name and title of "The Republic of Biafra". And I do declare that-

I. All political ties between us and the Federal Republic of Nigeria are hereby totally dissolved;

ii. All subsisting contractual obligations entered into by the Government of the Federal Republic of Nigeria or by any person, authority or organization or government acting on its behalf, with any person, authority or organization operating, or relating to any matter or thing, within the Republic of Biafra, shall henceforth be deemed to be entered into with the Military Governor of the Republic of Biafra for and on behalf of the Government and people of the republic of Biafra, and the covenants thereof shall, subject to this Declaration, be performed by the parties according to their tenor;

iii. All subsisting international treaties and obligations made on behalf of eastern Nigeria by the Government of the Federal

Republic of Nigeria, shall be honored and respected;

iv. Eastern Nigeria's due share of all subsisting international debits and obligations entered into by the Government of the Federal Republic of Nigeria on behalf of the Federation of Nigeria shall be honored and respected;

v. Steps will be taken to open discussions of the question of Eastern Nigeria's due share of the assets of the Federation of Nigeria and personal properties of the citizens of Biafra throughout the Federation of Nigeria;

vi. The rights, privileges, pensions, etc. of all personnel of the Public Services, the Armed Forces and the Police now serving in any capacity within the Republic of Biafra, are hereby guaranteed;

vii. We shall keep the door open for association with, and would welcome, any sovereign unit or units in the former Federation of Nigeria or in any other parts of Africa desirous of association with us for the purposes of running a common services organization and for the establishment of economic ties;

viii. We shall protect the lives and properties of all foreigners residing in Biafra; we shall extend the hand of friendship to those nations who respect our sovereignty, and shall repel any interference in our internal affairs;

ix. We shall faithfully adhere to the charter of the Organization of African Unity and of the United Nations Organization;

x. It is our intention to remain a member of the British Commonwealth of Nations in our right as a sovereign, independent nation.

Long live the Republic of Biafra! And may God protect all who live in her!

....

The Nigerian government refused to prevent the pogrom against Igbos, and in some cases encouraged and participated in the pogrom. Ojukwu could not stand and watch his people being killed while the state security apparatus nudged on the perpetrators. Fighting against a state that failed to protect a section of her citizenry is an unquestionably act of love!

He sacrifices the risk of losing his investment at Lagos for defending his people. Like God, he cares for his choosing people more than anything or all other people.

Moses couldn't stand the suffering of his people, so he rose against the oppressor and killed an Egyptian, which was an unquestionable act of love.

David couldn't stand against the humiliation of his people by Goliath, so he rose against him. That was an unquestionable act of love.

Elijah couldn't stand against the worship of foreign God, so he rose against BAAL and its prophets.

These were true men of God; they showed love and defended their people. They were not preachers or pastors. Which pastor today rises against the killing of Christians or his people? Answer that question for yourself.

"Because the black man is considered inferior and servile to the white, he must accept his political, social and economic system and ideologies ready made from Europe, America or the Soviet Union? Within the confines of his nation he must accept a federation or confederation or unitary government if federation or confederation or unitary government suits the interests of his white masters: he must accept inept and unimaginative leadership because the contrary would hurt the interests of the master race: he must accept economic exploitation by alien commercial firms and companies because the whites benefit from it. Beyond the confines of his state, he must accept regional and continental organizations, which provide a front for the manipulations of the imperialist powers: organizations, which are therefore unable to respond to African problems in a truly African manner. For Africans to show a true independence is to ask for anathematization and total liquidation".
Chukwuemeka Odumegwu Ojukwu,

When anything beyond the ordinary man's knowledge is revealed, it is always said to be divine. When one pastor proclaimed the activities of witchcraft against you, you believe it as divine even when witchcraft does not actually exist.

Ojukwu revealed the true enemy of the black man and her various strategies to ensure that the black man perpetually remains in chain. This was an act of divine care, an act of providence.

"Since in the thinking of many white powers, a good, progressive and efficient government is good only for whites, our view was considered dangerous and pernicious: a point of view which explains but does not justify the blind support which those powers have given to uphold the Nigerian ideal of a corrupt, decadent and putrefying society. To them genocide is an appropriate answer to any group of Black people who have the temerity to attempt to evolve their own social system". Chukwuemeka Odumegwu Ojukwu.
This was exactly what happened at Libya.
Under veracity, we further reveal the divine care and providence of Ojukwu.
Veracity simple means truthfulness.
"In the face of the movement for Negro freedom, the white imperialists changed their tactics. They decided to install puppet African administrations to create the illusion of political independence, while retaining the control of the economy. And this they quickly did between 1957 and 1965. The direct empire was transformed into an indirect empire, that regime of fraud and exploitation, which African nationalists aptly describe as neo-colonialism". Chukwuemeka Odumegwu Ojukwu.

"Nigeria was a classic example of neo-colonialist state. The militant nationalism of the late forties and early fifties had caught the British imperialists unawares. They hurried to accommodate it by installing the ignorant, decadent and feudalistic Hausa-Fulani oligarchy in power. For the British, the credentials of the Hausa-Fulani were that not having emerged from the middle ages they knew nothing about the modern state and the powerful forces that now rule men's minds. Owing their position to the British, they were servile and submissive. The result was that while Nigerians lived in the illusion of independence, they were still in fact being ruled from Number 10 Downing Street. The British still enjoyed a strangle hold on their economy". Chukwuemeka Odumegwu Ojukwu.

"The crises, which rocked Nigeria from the morrow of 'independence', were brought about by the efforts of progressive nationalists to achieve true independence for themselves and for posterity. For their part in this effort, Biafrans were stigmatized and singled out for extermination. In imperialist thinking, only phony independence is good for blacks. The sponsorship of Nigeria by white imperialism has not been disinterested. They are only concerned with the preservation of that corrupt and rickety structure of Nigeria in a perpetual state of powerlessness to check foreign exploitation" Chukwuemeka Odumegwu Ojukwu.

Is there anything far from the truth in the above quotes? We all know that we are dependent nations, our economy is controlled by foreign companies representing foreign interest, our culture is foreign and we are subservient to other part of the world.

Ojukwu as a true man of God was speaking the truth, risking his life on the process. Jesus Christ spoke the truth and payed with his life. Your pastor never spoke against the killing and the present state of Libya, they never lifted a finger against the imminent sponsors of Boko Haram, they never spoke during the Abacha regime in Nigeria, they indulge all politicians despite their track record, they never speak against neo-colonialism, they never studied the economic intrigues of the world because they are busy defrauding people in the name of Jesus.

Ojukwu was already a millionaires, his father's inheritance were mostly at Lagos which he know will not be part of Biafra meaning that he may lose them. He decided to fight for the liberation of his people using his personal money, something which majority of today's acclaimed men of God will never do. Ojukwu gave to his people but today men of God collect from their people and never give back.

Oxford-educated Chukwuemeka Odumegwu Ojukwu joined the Nigerian army, against his wealthy father's wishes, hoping to play an integral role in the nation's affairs once Nigeria had gained independence from Britain. He was always thinking ahead of time.

"Our revolution recognizes the importance of the mental and emotional need of the Biafran people. To this end, the Biafran state will pay great attention to education, culture and the arts. We shall aim at elevating our cultural institutions and promoting educational reforms, which will foster a sense of national and racial pride among our people and discourage ideas, which inspire a sense of inferiority and dependence on foreigners. It will be the prime duty of the revolutionary Biafran state to eradicate illiteracy from our society, to guarantee free education to all Biafran children to a stage limited only by existing resources.

Our nation will encourage the training of scientists, technicians and skilled workers needed for quick industrialization and the modernization of our agriculture. We will ensure the development of higher education and technological training for our people, encourage our intellectuals, writers, artists and scientists to research, create and invent in the service of the state and the people. We must prepare our people to contribute significantly to knowledge and world culture." Chukwuemeka Odumegwu Ojukwu.

Ojukwu recognized that the basic need of the Biafran people is mental revolution. Your pastor never recognize your need, he emerge you in fake spirituality to the extend you forget the world around you. You need earth more than heaven.

"...Having mandated me to proclaim on your behalf, and in your name, that Eastern Nigeria be a sovereign independent Republic,

Now, therefore, I, Lieutenant-Colonel Chukwuemeka Odumegwu Ojukwu, Military Governor of Eastern Nigeria, by virtue of the authority, and pursuant to the principles, recited above, do hereby solemnly proclaim that the territory and region known as and called Eastern Nigeria together with her continental shelf and territorial waters shall henceforth be an independent sovereign state of the name and title of "The Republic of Biafra".

I always ask people this question, what vision is your pastor actually leading? Promise of heaven, miracle and prosperity seem to be the only vision. Then I ask, how exactly does it impact on your life *directly*? I italicized directly, because people unknowing give out credit from their hard work to God and their pastors while in reality, their achievement is 100% the product of their hard work. If your pastor actually lead a vision that benefit you, the benefit should directly come from the vision not some 'miraculous way' relating to your business or work.

Ojukwu led a vision of creating a modern African state that will be truly independent.

Each time I peruse General Ojukwu's manifesto for the Biafran state, I deduce: this is a man who saw tomorrow, a man that knew Nigeria well and wanted freedom for his people, to explore their potentials and become the pride of every black man anywhere in the world. Today, the north still killed the south. Today, the wealth from the south is used to develop the north while the south wallows in poverty. Today the imperialist still hold a tight grip on our economy. Today the black man is still subservient to other race, today racist power still topple African government that does not play to their rule. Today decisions and appointments are still marked base on tribal and religious affiliation in Nigeria and Africa.

All these Ojukwu foresaw before anyone else was able. He was an embodiment of God. God said to pharaoh let my people go and we applaud it, Ojukwu said to Nigeria let my people go and we tag him evil. Where is the justice?

"We in Biafra are convinced that the black man can never come into his own until he is able to build modern states based on indigenous African ideologies, to enjoy true independence, to be able to make his mark in the arts and sciences and to engage in meaningful dialogue with the white man on a basis of equality. When he achieves this, he will have brought a new dimension into international affairs. Biafra will not betray the black man. No matter the odds, we will fight with all our might until black men everywhere can point with pride to this republic, standing dignified and defiant, an example of African nationalism triumphant over its many and age-old enemies". Chukwuemeka Odumegwu Ojukwu.

"We believe that human effort and will are necessary to bring about changes and improvements in the condition of the individual and society. The Biafran would, thus, make the effort to improve his lot and the material well-being of his community. He has the will to transform his society into a modern progressive community. In this process of rapid transformation he will retain and cherish the best elements of his culture, drawing sustenance as well as moral and psychological stability from them. But being a Biafran he will never be afraid to adapt what needs to be adapted or challenge what has to be changed.

The Biafran revolution will continue to discover and develop local

talent and to use progressive foreign ideas and skills so long as they do not destroy the identity of our culture or detract from the sovereignty of our fatherland. The Biafran revolution will also ensure through education that the positive aspects of Biafran traditional culture, especially those which are likely to be swamped out of existence by introducing foreign influence. The undiscriminating absorption of new ideas and attitudes will be discouraged".
Chukwuemeka Odumegwu Ojukwu.
"We accepted by this revolutionary act, the glory, as well as the sacrifice, of true independence and freedom. We knew that we had challenged the many forces and interests, which had conspired to keep Africa and the black race in subjection forever. We knew they were going to be ruthless and implacable in defense of their age-old imposition on us and exploitation of our people. But we were prepared, and remain prepared, to pay any price for our freedom and dignity" Chukwuemeka Odumegwu Ojukwu.

Ojukwu rose against powerful forces and remained alive. Hitler attempted it but was never found, Jesus Christ attempted it and was killed, Patrice Lumumba attempted it and was killed etc. Ojukwu was omnipotent.

PRESENT AFRICAN MEN OF GOD
Search and you will find them, they are not pulpit preachers, they preach and practice true independence of Africa; an economic, political, technological, religious and cultural independence.

They called for an all-African referendum which will lead to the emerging of true African nations not the contraption created by Europe, these true nations can unit to form an African union government with limited power; armed forces, police, science and technology duplicated at the union government level and the constituent state(true nations) level. A unify foreign policy will be adopted throughout the entire African nation.

They believe the people should exercise their will, no body, no human have the power to choose association for others, nature endorsed in everyone's freedom; freedom of choice, freedom of associations, freedom of believe.

They are ardent believers of pan-Africanism. They protest against the importation of any goods or services that is produce in the country. They practice protectionism.

They are like Moses and David, they are not religious leaders, they are true liberators, they are the Patrice Lumumba of Congo and Ojukwu of Biafra. They know religion is one of the problem in Africa and never a solution to a single problem.

They know that Africa is on the tight creep of imperialism and neo-colonialism and work to eradicate all form of dependency. They believe with science and technology independence, with economic independence, with legal independence, with cultural independence, Africa will be losing from the shackle of imperialism and neo-colonialism.

They propagate, preach and practice self-independence, self-reliance and self-sufficience. They don't believe in miracle because nature never deviates from its laws. They experience the true power of God, a realist God; nature.

They know that science is the true study of God and technology is the only true miracle. They work tirelessly to produce technology in their country. They equally patronize indigenous technology.

They don't condone corruption nor welcome corrupt official in their 'ministry', they speak and rise against corruption and injustice. They fight with arms just like Moses, David, Elijah, and Elisha to liberate their people.

They help the poor in the society instead of collecting from them in the name of God. They contribute positively to the development of the society instead of only taking from them.

They believe in brotherhood, a natural line of relation. They are like the Jews, ancient mafia; they build everything around their family, around their tribe, around their race.

Watch out, you will see them; they are the true men of God.

CHAPTER THREE

GOOD VERSUS EVIL
THE REALITY

THE TRUE EVIL

Religion has actually convinced people to believe in absurdities. One of such absurdity is their definition of good and evil (sin).

Religion makes people believed that there is a place prepared for them when they die, that sex before marriage is sin, that telling lies is sin, that associating with unbelievers is sin, that hatred is sin, that killing is sin, that there is God's divine plan for everyone, that God has a hand in human affairs, that God can do all things. Etc.

Religious definition of what is right and what is wrong is based on wrong premise which is inconsistence with the truth because God carried out or supported these act.

God said this is my people and killed the Canaanites to give the Israelite their land and he is praised. Hitler said we are the master race and wiped out people and he was called evil. Religion does not allow reasoning and free will to prevail.

The context in which these acts are undertaking is actually the sin not the act itself. In legal system, if you killed for self-defense, you may be discharged and acquitted or charged for man slaughter not murder. The context, the circumstance and the motive of the killing determine if you committed sin (crime) or not. This is the reality.

If you are oppressed by a people; they rape your women, cart away your properties and killed your men. One day, you are opportune to kill them, is that a sin?

Abraham lied to save his life by claiming his wife to be his sister. This was not considered a sin in the bible because he did it to save his life.

God divinely impregnated Mary to give birth to Jesus without marriage; this was not considered a sin in the bible. Moreover, in reality, two people have to test their compatibility before marriage.

Moses killed an Egyptian and thousands more were drawn by God himself. David killed goliath, these were not considered sin in the bible.

Jesus associated himself with sinners and tax collectors, he said, I came for the sinners.

Now, why do we now believe all theses to be sin? Religion is the answer.

Religion is designed to make people docile, ignorant, gullible and dependent. It provides succor for the weak, instrument for the oppressor and tool for control of the foolish.

It actually propagates the real sin and misleads the people, focusing their attention on irrelevant things while propagating the real sin.

What is truly evil?

The greatest evil on mankind is religion. Don't get this wrong, religion as it is currently practice, both Christianity and Islam is the problem. Religion that preaches freedom and independent, that preaches science and technology is not the problem.

TYPES AND EFFECT OF EVIL MESSAGES
God-reliant messages

This gospel ascribes everything to God; everything is spiritual or has some spiritual connotation and must be treated as such. Issues that ought to be treated by a professional are handled by the church. The churches of today are hospital for the sick, consultancy firm for those who seek knowledge, school for the uneducated and house of hope for the hopeless.

God-reliant messages emphasizes that men should rely on God for everything because God have plans and answers to all of us. Emphatically, this gospel advice men to stop thinking, to stop being creative, to stop reasoning, to stop being productive, to stop working as God alone will do everything for them.

God-reliant messages crumble a society and render it poor and underdeveloped because all ancient and present civilization was created by human NOT GOD. The city of Babaal was built by men not God. Men build the develop nations of today not God. The temple of Solomon was built by men.

The bible book of Matthew 6;25-28, said that we should not think of tomorrow for the bird neither sow nor reap but yet they eat. This is used in support of this gospel.

However, nature provided us with brain to perform many functions among them, the ability to think and solve problems, the ability to think and create new things but the God-reliant messages is taking this away from us and killing the gift of nature in human.

This is evil, one of the greatest to befall a people. A generation that rely on God for virtually everything is bound to fail.

Prosperity message

This gospel ascribe prosperity to God, it says that so far you attend church, pay your tithe, automatically, you will be wealthy. This gospel is designed to draw people to church and to fill the coffer of the church founder who wittily show case himself as testimony of God's blessing while actually, the members are the source of his blessing. Wealthy pastors are those with large congregation and network of branches. Think, does manna ever fall from heaven?

Wealth is a product of good financial education, this is the truth. The prosperity message gives hope in a hopeless society but it fails to state that hope can never be fulfilled without plan. It renders the people hopeful and faithful. Hope and faith are fine attributes but only when they are backed with the right information, plan and strategy which the messages never provide. Those that strive to be a little bit real still attach the God-reliant message to it, this killed the fact. Giving people hope without the right back up is tantamount to nothing. This message equally crumbles the thinking and creative ability of the society, it makes the people dependents and poor. This is evil, a sin.

Harvest and seed time message

Harvest and seed time is in consonant with natural laws. You must sow to reap but the context in which the fake churches present this universal truth is the issue here.

They want you to sow in the church not in your brain, to sow to your pastor's life not your community. They make you believed that it is only by sowing in the church that God will bless you. In reality, you can sow into anybody's life and still ripe, it must not be in the church.

A church that preaches tithe and offering as a sermon, a church that never speaks of orphanage, destitute and indigent student, a church that never speak against corruption in the society is never of God, it is of the devil.

Sow into your mentality.

Miracle message

This is the best optical illusion I have ever seen, nature never deviate from its set rules. There is no miracle but manifestation, adoption or manipulation of natural laws.

Helicopter is sustained on air against gravity, is that a miracle or manipulation of natural law?

With the discovery of radio waves, man is able to communicate wireless across ocean, is that a miracle or manifestation of natural law? Radio waves was always there to assist invisible communication, it's discovery and adoption does not constitute a miracle.

If man discovers the magnetic character of the human mind which in reality exist as the foundation of all 'miracle', and uses it to display what no man has ever seen, does that constitute a miracle? Absolutely NO! It is simple the adoption of natural law because it has being in existent. The man only discovers how to make use of it. Think.

This fake men of God sometime stage manage event, pray and things which would have still been without the prayer becomes and they proclaimed it miracle, no it is optical illusion grounded on probability.

Nature is govern by laws which permit the human mind to magnet her dominant thought, laws which return negative for negative and positive for positive (Karmas), laws which sustain a dying man with an insurmountable desire to live, laws which release hormones to the body to heal a sickness when the mind is stimulated, laws that blessed those vested in knowledge above those who are not.

There is no miracle, don't be ignorant, nature consist of everything, things beyond your wildest imagination. When men who seek and acquire knowledge play on nature, don't be astonish for you can do the same if not that you are ignorant, indifferent, mentally enslaved and non-ambitious.

The miracle message is the greatest evil in Africa. When other part of the world are building supersonic air plane, we are busy believing that witchcraft fly at night. When other part of the world carried out organs transplant, we are busy hoping for a miraculous healing. When other parts of the world are busy building weapons, we are here hoping for divine protection.

Baseless possibility message

This message is the summation of all other messages, it is based on the presumption that everything is possible through Christ Jesus.

For years, we cannot alleviate poverty in Africa through Christ Jesus, we cannot refine our natural resources through Christ Jesus, we don't have steady electrical power through Christ Jesus, and we cannot heal everyone and close down all hospitals through Christ Jesus.

Like every other fake prophet messages, they always express universal truth in a wrong context. There is no impossibility in life; the only thing that can stop men from acquiring, discovering, building, and creating whatever they desire is time. Time is the only natural phenomenon that can stop a man not your believed or disbelief in Christ. The best inventors and scientist in the world were/are artists.

With infinite time, a man who set his goal and work toward it under the influence of a motive, if he has a million years to go in a definite direction, nothing can stop him even when he desires to create a human being with complete blood, brain and organs of a biological person. Don't doubt me, we are part of God, we are part of nature.

Natural law says that whatever the mind of man conceive, believe, and work towards it with motive and practical plan, the forces of nature will bring to his disposal the circumstance of life, resources, people and knowledge needed to accomplish such goal as you work towards it, the only hindrance is time. This is the law governing the magnetic character of the human mind. For your pastor to say you need Christ Jesus, that is a lie.

NATIONAL SIN

The undeveloped countries otherwise called third world are the most evil countries in the world. Surprisingly, they are the most religious. Shouldn't the presence of God equate with their level of development? Countries, especially African countries who love and worship God, shouldn't God look down on them, open the window of heaven and develop them? On the contrary, this never happened and will never happen because men develop their society not God.

Africans are worshiping evil and ignorance, and ignore the right thing; good and reality. Science is the only true study of God while technology is the only miracle. These third world countries are worshiping imaginary, illusion, non-existence and the most despicable fiction of all time, which is the greatest evil to befall a nation.

A nation that cannot extract and refine her natural resources but rather export the raw and import the finish product is evil. They ignore the search for the true God; science and wallop for an imaginary God.

A nation that consume technology more than it produce is evil. They refuse the search for true miracle; technology and follow imaginary, stage manage and cheap magic.

A nation that does not intervene and support an act of innovation in any part of the country is evil. They choose to partner with their imperial masters and crumble the home industry.

A nation that does not outlaw the importation of anything which can be locally produced in the country is evil.

A nation that conspires with western nation or Europe to fight his people is evil.

A nation that stock away it's wealth in foreign bank is evil

A nation that is more than 50% technological dependent; whose construction, mining, drilling, building of power station and railway are handled by foreign companies is evil.

A nation whose citizen cannot handle its technological need; construction of roads, bridge, railways, power station, drilling and mining of natural resources in their land, refining of the natural resources etc. is full of evil people.

A nation whose majority of its citizen hopes on miracle is doom.

The misinterpretation of good and evil by religious people is always beclouded by ignorance and religious stupidity. Open your eye, look around, what has religion actually done to the society? What development is religion adding to Africa?

A nation that suppresses the aspiration and will of the people for association and self-determination is of evil. Is there any greater evil more than what I just mentioned?

Sex matters, evangelism, entertainment, football etc. are not things we should discuss, we as a people should focus on eradicating the above national evil.

NATIONAL GOOD

The preaching and practice of self-independence, self-reliance and self-sufficience is the true word of God.

What is an independent nation? It is a nation founded by the will and aspiration of the people which is technology, religious, political, economic and cultural self-reliant.

This definition called for explanation of some terms:

THE WILL AND ASPIRATION OF THE PEOPLE

An independent nation must be founded base on agreement of the majority of the constituting people through a referendum, separatism war and tribal affiliation.

Any nation put together by a conqueror is not a true nation but remains a conquered territory even after the declaration of political independence. This is because the economic, military (technology), religious and cultural independence is not declared or taking. Political independence became weak in the present of technology, culture, religious and economic dependence.

A true nation must truly be independent.

ECONOMIC SELF-RELIANCE OR INDEPENDENCE

This simple means exporting more of machineries, knowledge, technology, consumer's goods and services and importing more raw materials and semi finish goods.

That is simple and that is true economic self-reliance. Forget all complex economic theory they taught you. This is the summary of what it takes to be economically independent as a nation.

POLITICAL SELF-RELIANCE OR INDEPENDENCE

This simply means the number and strength of international organizations founded and controlled by Africa to the ratio controlled by other blocks.

As usual, it is as simple as that, don't be deceived by any expert or professor or the so called international organization.

Africa should do away with some organizations and form true African union, African armed forces, African world trade regulating authority, African criminal court, African monetary zone/bank, African central intelligent agency, African news network etc.

TECHNOLOGY SELF-RELIANCE OR INDEPENDENCE

This is simply the ability to manufacture by ourselves; sophisticated arms, machines and technological based products and services.

Always simple yet it holds the ultimate truth.

CULTURAL SELF-RELIANCE OR INDEPENDENCE

Culture is the total way of life of the people not some traditional dance or event.

Here is our current culture as a people:

a)   Presently, Africans created enemy among themselves and seek foreign help to fight among themselves.

b)   Africans seek for foreign investments and did nothing to protect the local investments in existent.

c)   Africans seek foreign aids to buy drugs and other things from the very nations that supply the aids and to develop infrastructure, contracting foreign companies.

d)   African leaders concentrate in developing infrastructure such as road, water, building of schools, market, railway etc., with 90% foreign technology.

e) Africans elites fly abroad for medical treatment and send their kids to schools abroad.
f) Africans believe that government should solve our entire problems.
g) Africans play much of domestic politics and virtually have no voice in international politics.
h) Africans are inferior on the world scene, anything the white man does is ok; anything a fellow black man does, calls for scrutiny.
i) Africans believe much on supernatural solutions than technological solutions.
j) Africans are not patriotic, maybe their current individual countries are not true nations.
k) Africans disdain everything indigenous and embraces everything foreign.
l) Africans love other races more than we love ourselves.
m) Africans love foreign products more than indigenous products.
n) Africans believe that nothing good can and will come out of their country.

Cultural self-reliance is a change from our current ways of life as listed above to the exact opposite. Write down the exact opposite of these cultural tread in Africa and you will understand the true meaning of cultural self-reliance.

When a true man of God rise just as Moses who saved the Israelites from Egypt, David who saved the Israelites from the philistines, Elijah which saved his religion from Baal; he will be persecuted just like Moses, David, Elijah, Abraham and all true men of God. This is a sign that you are dealing with a true liberator.

A true man of God drives toward total independence and self-reliance, he is one who put himself in precarious position; whose national boarder will be sealed and sanction impose, membership of some international organization terminated, sanction or attack by some countries or organizations who never want us to rise, who believed on some absurdities.

They will use frivolous excuses or maybe even uses a set up covert operation to buy the public support. True men of God will suffer as a people, and then finally evolve as a free people, totally independent and self-reliant.

This is why Africa need to be free, to become developed nations. This is what all men of God went through; Moses ran out of Egypt, Elijah was hunted, David was hunted by Saul. All true men of God face prosecution. Even Jesus himself was persecuted.

Today the present men of God are not persecuted because they are not preaching the true message of God; the deliverance and emancipation of their people. Watch out for the message of God has arrived!

CHARACTERISTIC OF A GODLY MAN

A Godly man lives for the glory of his people not for personal glory; he lives for a greater reward. A Godly man like Moses, David, Elijah and others are always those who stood up and fought for a course greater than themselves.

For even the Son of Man did not come to be served, but to serve, and to give His life a ransom for many." —Mark 10:45

He Love his people above all and is ready to die for them just as Christ died for his people.

A Godly man stands for self-reliance and true independence of his people. He live and propagate economic, political, cultural, religious and technology independence.

He seeks economic power for his people.

Which pastor today is ready to give his life for the liberation of his people from oppressive regime?

CHARACTERISTIC OF A SINFUL MAN

A sinful man does not step up to help his society nor speak out in the mist of evil. Fela kuti of Nigeria was more of a Godly man than many so called men of God today because they never spoke out in the mist of evil. Fela was persecuted.

A sinful man is he who believes God will solve all his problems and rely on the west for help when actually the west is exploiting them. He believes that he can never produce technology and does not support, patronize or protect local technology.

A sinful man lives for himself and exploit the people for his own benefit. They live as celebrities with luxury life style, owns private jet and careless of his followers.

A sinful man stand for nothing, he has no societal goal and solely a pure capitalist.

A sinful man propagate the ideology of heaven and hell, he want you to suffer on earth with the hope that God has prepare a luxury place for you in heaven.

WHO IS YOUR PASTOR

Is your pastor a true man of God or religious leader? Maybe you should read again from the beginning; this time with a pen and paper, list down the quality of a true man of God and that of false men of God or religious leaders and compare with your pastor, only then will you discover the truth because truth that is self-revealing is more believable than what you are told.

Answer those questions with reference to your pastor.

Then I ask again, who is your pastor, is he truly a man of God?

CHAPTER FOUR

WHAT/WHO IS GOD?

RELIGIOUS DEFINITION OF GOD

Judaism[10] is the oldest monotheistic faith. It affirms the existence of one God, **Yahweh,** who entered into covenant with the descendants of Abraham, God's chosen people. Judaism's holy writings reveal how God has been present with them throughout their history. These writings are known as the Torah, specifically the five books of Moses, but most broadly conceived as the Hebrew Scriptures (traditionally called the Old Testament by Christians) and the compilation of oral tradition known as the Talmud (which includes the Mishnah, the oral law).

According to Scripture, the Hebrew patriarch, Abraham (20th century B.C.) founded the faith that would become known as Judaism. He obeyed the call of God to depart northern Mesopotamia and travel to Canaan. God promised to bless his descendants if they remained faithful in worship. Abraham's line descended through Isaac, then Jacob (also called Israel; his descendants came to be called Israelites). According to Scripture, 12 families that descended from Jacob migrated to Egypt, where they were enslaved. They were led out of bondage (13th century B.C.) by Moses, who united them in the worship of Yahweh. The Hebrews returned to Canaan after a 40-year sojourn in the desert, conquering from the local peoples the "promised land" that God had provided for them.....

Christianity

Christianity[11] is a monotheistic religion founded by the followers of **Jesus of Nazareth, the Christ.** Jesus, a Jew, was born in about 7 B.C. and assumed his public life, probably after his 30th year, in Galilee. The New Testament Gospels describe Jesus as a teacher and miracle worker. He proclaimed the kingdom of God, a future reality that is at the same time already present. Jesus set the requirements for participation in the kingdom of God as a change of heart and repentance for sins, love of God and neighbor, and concern for justice. Circa A.D. 30 he was executed on a cross in Jerusalem, a brutal form of punishment for those considered a political threat to the Roman Empire.

After his death his followers came to believe in him as the Christ, the Messiah. The Gospels report his resurrection and how the risen Jesus was witnessed by many of his followers. The apostle Paul helped spread the new faith in his missionary travels. Historically, Christianity arose out of Judaism and claims that Jesus fulfilled many of the promises of the Hebrew Scripture (often referred to as the Old Testament).

The new religion spread rapidly throughout the Roman Empire. In its first two centuries, Christianity began to take shape as an organization, developing distinctive doctrine, liturgy, and ministry. By the fourth century the Christian church had taken root in countries stretching from Spain in the West to Persia and India in the East.

Christians had been subject to persecution by the Roman state, but gained tolerance under Constantine the Great (A.D. 313). The church became favored under his successors, and in 380 AD the emperor Theodosius proclaimed Christianity the state religion. Other religions were suppressed.

Because differences in doctrine threatened to divide the church, a standard Christian creed was formulated by bishops at successive ecumenical councils, the first of which was held in A.D. 325 (Nicaea). Important doctrines were defined concerning the Trinity-in other words, that there is one God in three persons: Father, Son, and Holy Spirit (Constantinople, A.D. 381), and the nature of Christ as both divine and human (Chalcedon, A.D. 541). Christians came to accept both Hebrew Scripture and the New Testament as authoritative. The New Testament comprises four Gospels (narratives of Jesus' life), 21 Epistles, The Acts of the Apostles, and Revelation.

Jesus claimed to be the son of God and said no one can come to the father except through him.

Today, Christianity is divided into many sects and denomination each with a different view of God. They are;

The orthodox (Catholics) this sect believe in God the father, his son, the mother of God Mary and all saint as divine. They are conservative. The female members cover their head and are not allowed to put on trousers.

The Inventors (Mormons, Jehovah Witness, brotherhood of the cross and star, etc.) these are people who reinvented Christianity and added their idea to it. Mormon wrote their modern Bible,

Jehovah witness called God JEHOVAH, Brotherhood sees their leader, Olumba Olumba Obu as the personification of God.

The Pentecostal or modern Christian (liberal) this sect of Christian worship JESUS as their God. They are shaped by the society and sometime worship their pastors. For them, materialism is the ultimate blessing from God. Dressing and dance steps are not regulated, they sometime play an edited secular music. They perform or claim to perform miracle.

Spiritual churches (Medieval Mysticism) this church inculcate African traditional worship into their doctrine. They burn incense, offer sacrifice, and perform other ritual. To them God is spirit.

Islam

One[12] of the three major monotheistic faiths, was founded in Arabia by Muhammad between 610 and 632(AC). There are an estimated 4.6 million Muslims in North America and 1.57 billion Muslims worldwide.

Muhammad was born in A.D. 570 at Mecca and belonged to the Quraysh tribe, which was active in the caravan trade. At the age of 25 he joined the trade from Mecca to Syria in the employment of a rich widow, Khadija, whom he later married. Critical of the lax moral standards and polytheistic practices of the inhabitants of Mecca, he began to lead a contemplative life in the desert. In a dramatic religious vision, the angel Gabriel announced to Muhammad that he was to be a prophet. Encouraged by Khadija, he devoted himself to the reform of religion and society. Polytheism was to be abandoned. But leaders of the Quraysh generally rejected his teaching, and Muhammad gained only a small following and suffered persecution. He eventually fled Mecca.

The Hegira (Hijra, meaning "emigration") of Muhammad from Mecca, where he was not honored, to Medina, where he was well received, occurred in 622 and marks the beginning of the Muslim era. After a number of military conflicts with Mecca, in 630 he marched on Mecca and conquered it. Muhammad died at Medina in 632. His grave there has since been a place of pilgrimage.

Muhammad's followers, called Muslims, revered him as the prophet of **Allah (God);** the only God. Muslims consider Muhammad to be the last in the line of prophets that included Abraham and Jesus. Islam spread quickly, stretching from Spain in the west to India in the east within a century after the prophet's death. Sources of the Islamic faith are the Qur'an (Koran), regarded as the uncreated, eternal Word of God, and tradition (hadith) regarding sayings and deeds of the prophet.

Islam means "surrender to the will of Allah," the all-powerful, who determines humanity's fate. Good deeds will be rewarded at the Last Judgment in paradise, and evil deeds will be punished in hell.

The Five Pillars, or primary duties, of Islam are profession of faith; prayer, to be performed five times a day; alms giving to the poor and the mosque (house of worship); fasting during daylight hours in the month of Ramadan; and pilgrimage to Mecca (the hajj) at least once in a Muslim's lifetime, if it is physically and financially possible. The pilgrimage includes homage to the ancient shrine of the Ka'aba, the most sacred site in Islam.

Muslims gather for corporate worship on Fridays. Prayers and sermon take place at the mosque, which is also a center for teaching of the Qur'an. The community leader, the imam, is considered a teacher and prayer leader.

Islam succeeded in uniting an Arab world of separate tribes and castes, but disagreements concerning the succession of the prophet caused a division in Islam between two groups, Sunnis and Shi'ites. The Shi'ites rejected the first three successors to Muhammad as usurpers, claiming the fourth, Muhammad's son-in-law Ali, as the rightful leader. The Sunnis (from the word tradition), the largest division of Islam (today more than 87%), believe in the legitimacy of the first three successors. Among these, other sects arose (such as the conservative Wahhabi of Saudi Arabia), as well as different schools of theology. Another development within Islam, begins in the eighth and ninth centuries, was Sufism, a form of mysticism. This movement was influential for many centuries and was instrumental in the spread of Islam in Asia and Africa.

Islam has expanded greatly under Muhammad's successors. It is the principal religion of the Middle East, Asia, and the northern half of Africa.

Buddhism

Buddhism was[13] founded in the fourth or fifth century B.C. in northern India by a man known traditionally as Siddhartha meaning "he who has reached the goal" Gautama, the son of a warrior prince. Some scholars believe that he lived from 563 to 483 B.C., though his exact life span is uncertain. Troubled by the inevitability of suffering in human life, he left home and a pampered life at the age of 29 to wander as an ascetic, seeking religious insight and a solution to the struggles of human existence. He passed through many trials and practiced extreme self-denial. Finally, while meditating under the bodhi tree ("tree of perfect knowledge"), he reached enlightenment and taught his followers about his new spiritual understanding. At the core of his understanding were the Four Noble Truths: (1) all living beings suffer; (2) the origin of this suffering is desire material possessions, power, and so on; (3) desire can be overcome; and (4) there is a path that leads to release from desire. This way is called the Noble Eightfold Path: right views, right intention, right speech, right action, right livelihood, right effort, right concentration, and right ecstasy.

Gautama promoted the concept of anatman (that a person has no actual self) and the idea that existence is characterized by impermanence. This realization helps one let go of desire for transient things. Still, Gautama did not recommend extreme self-denial but rather a disciplined life called the Middle Way. Like the Hindus, he believed that existence consisted of reincarnation, a cycle of birth and death. He held that it could be broken only by reaching complete detachment from worldly cares. Then the soul could be released into nirvana (literally "blowing out")

indescribable state of total transcendence. Gautama traveled to preach the dharma (sacred truth) and was recognized as the Buddha (enlightened one). After his death his followers continued to develop doctrine and practice, which came to center on the Three Jewels: the dharma (the sacred teachings of Buddhism), the sangha (the community of followers, which now includes nuns, monks, and laity), and the Buddha.

Numerous Buddhist sects have emerged. The oldest, called the Theravada (Way of the Elders) tradition, interprets Buddha as a great sage but not a deity. It emphasizes meditation and ritual practices that help the individual become an arhat, an enlightened being. Its followers emphasize the authority of the earliest Buddhist scriptures, the Tripitaka (Three Baskets), a compilation of sermons, rules for celibates, and doctrine. This sect is prevalent in Southeast Asia and Sri Lanka. It is sometimes called the Hinayana (Lesser Vehicle) tradition (once considered a pejorative term).

Between the second century B.C. and the second century A.D., the Mahayana (Greater Vehicle) tradition refocused Buddhism to concentrate less on individual attainment of enlightenment and more on concern for humanity. It promotes the ideal of the bodhisattva (enlightened being), who shuns entering nirvana until all sentient beings can do so as well, willingly remaining in the painful cycle of birth and death to perform works of compassion. Members of this tradition conceive of Buddha as an eternal being to whom prayers can be made; other Buddhas are revered as well, adding a polytheistic dimension to the religion. Numerous sects have developed from the Mahayana tradition, which has been influential in China, Korea, and Japan.

A third broad tradition, variously called Vajrayana (Diamond Vehicle), Mantrayana (Vehicle of the Mantra), or Tantric Buddhism, offers a quicker, more demanding way to achieve nirvana. Because of its level of challenge to reach enlightenment in one life time requires the guidance of a spiritual leader. It is most prominent in Tibet and Mongolia. Zen Buddhism encourages individuals to seek the Buddha nature within themselves and to practice a disciplined form of sitting meditation in order to reach satori-spiritual enlightenment.

SCIENTIST VIEW ABOUT GOD
The Darwin Tempest
Charles Darwin's theory of evolution set off a firestorm of controversy that continues even today. The concept of one species descending from another directly contradicted biblical creationism and was considered a godless explanation for life and man. The one time ministerial student wrote in a letter to John Fordyce in 1879 "I have never been an atheist in the sense of denying the existence of a God. —I think that... an agnostic would be the most correct description of my state of mind." So Darwin, by his own words, was an agnostic.

Max Planck Quantum Mechanic
Max Planck, German Physicist, founded Quantum Theory. Simply put this theory gave a tool for understanding atomic level activity and the influence of surrounding fields. Some claim this theory is where science and theology intersect. He was a Christian but did not condemn those who thought differently. He once said, "Religion is the link that binds man to God." Max Plank: Believe in God.

Albert Einstein Energy and Matter
Albert Einstein's philosophy about the supernatural is complicated and perhaps brilliant, like his theories in physics. His most telling statement was, "I believe in Spinoza's God who reveals himself in the orderly harmony of what exists, not in a God who concerns

himself with the fates and actions of human beings." Einstein seems to have rejected traditional religious views in favor of a force that gives order to the universe. We might call Einstein a "Deist" since he believed in some organizing power but completely rejected the idea of a personal God.

Edwin Hubble, the Expanding Universe
Edwin Hubble's work laid the foundation for the expanding universe theory and the resultant "Big Bang" theory of the creation of the universe. His other accomplishments in astronomy are also amazing. Galaxies existing beyond our own and redshift-distance relationship were also his contributions. Hubble was raised Christian and in some early letters alluded to the idea that he believed he had some sort of "destiny" which wasn't explained. Hubble's thoughts about God, if he had any, are unknown.

J. Robert Oppenheimer, Fan of Eastern Literature
J. Robert Oppenheimer, a physicist and scientific director of the Manhattan Project, was known to be interested in Eastern religions and he sometimes quoted from Eastern philosophy. He read the Bhagavad Gita while in college and was greatly impressed with it, but, aside from an intellectual interest there is no evidence that Oppenheimer believed in or practiced any religion. Whether Oppenheimer believed in a higher power in any form is unknown.

Edward Teller, The Ultimate Deterrent
Edward Teller, called the "Father of the H-Bomb" was an avowed agnostic with faith in technology, not a supreme being. Like many

of his contemporaries, he was driven by his work and gave little or no thought to God or philosophy. His Jewish background was virtually missing from his later life. Edward Teller was an agnostic.

James Watson, DNA Co-Discoverer
James Watson was half of the famed research team or Watson and Crick that unraveled the secrets of DNA. The results of his work have evolved into the advanced genetic research of today. Watson once told his students that, "he was a total believer in evolution" and feels the Bible is "just not right" in the face of science. He also confessed that he does not believe in a soul or anything divine. James Watson is an atheist.

Francis Crick, DNA Co-Discoverer
Francis Crick, the rest of the Watson and Crick team, was speaking to a reporter for The Telegraph and said: "The god hypothesis is rather discredited." He also once stated that his distaste for religion was a primary driving factor in his research, which he felt would debunk the God theory for good. Francis Crick, obviously, was an Atheist.

Carl Sagan, A Modern View
Carl Sagan, "The People's Astronomer," made many interesting statements about God. "The idea that God is an oversized white male with a flowing beard, who sits in the sky and tallies the fall of every sparrow is ludicrous. But if by God, one means the set of physical laws that govern the universe, then clearly there is such a God. This God is emotionally unsatisfying... it does not make much

sense to pray to the law of gravity." Sagan, however, denied that he was an atheist: "An atheist has to know a lot more than I know." In reply to a question in 1996 about his religious beliefs, Sagan answered, "I'm agnostic." By Carl Sagan's self-description, he was an agnostic.

Stephen hawking

Stephen Hawking, the most famed physicist alive today, once wrote that "the actual point of creation lies outside the scope of presently known laws of physics..." Is this a puzzling statement coming from someone who grew up in an atheist household?

In a perhaps more telling statement from Hawking he stated that "An expanding universe does not preclude a creator, but it does place limits on when he might have carried out his job!" It is well known by Hawking followers that he doesn't believe in God, at least not in any conventional sense.

We'll call it as being "reasonably certain" that Stephen Hawking is an atheist.

THE SEARCH

Mankind for age marvels at the wonders of the universe and has forever sought answers; the processes involves many field of studies and institutions such as science, philosophy, religion, astrology, mystic, power, economy, technology, history etc.

Of the entire fields, religion is mostly accepted as the only study of God, it claims to be an authority in the subject of God. This assertion is wrong for if religion is the ultimate answer, then there should be a universal religion, dogma or denomination, for it ought

to be only one truth in the subject of God, the universal truth.
Wikionart.org defines God in the following ways;
God is the single deity of various monotheists' religion.
God is the single male deity of various duo theistic religions.
God is an impersonal and universal spiritual presence or force.
God is an omnipotent being, creator of the universe (as in deism).
God is the (personification of the) laws of nature.
If the entire world does not propagate one God, which is not forced on the people but by the foundation of free will, which currently does not happened and will never happened, it implies many things: either God is not universal or God is not yet discovered.
A single truth will have wipe away the entire faulty religion by now because truth is undisputable. We all know this haven't happened and will never happened and continues formation of new religion and the incessant denomination of the existence religion point to a single fact; that mankind have not discovered God. What they presently worship is imaginary. Truth they said is relative, truth i said is sacrosanct.
What is truth? Truth is anything which can be proven beyond reasonable doubt to be real, correct, right and factual. No one till date has been able to prove the God concept beyond reasonable doubt.
In ancient time, the world was believed to be flat but when the truth emerges, it wipes away the flatness 'truth' of the time.
The fact that many religion and domination exist and God bears different names implies that the God theory is not a universal truth because one religious truth will have wiped out all other false

religion, just as one scientific truth always and will ever wipe off faulty theory.

WHAT OR WHO IS GOD
The ultimate question remains; what or who is God?
"Sometimes people hold a core belief that is very strong. When they are presented with evidence that works against that belief, the new evidence cannot be accepted. It would create a feeling that is extremely uncomfortable, called cognitive dissonance. And because it is so important to protect the core belief, they will rationalize, ignore and even deny anything that doesn't fit in with the core belief." **Frantz Fanon,**

That quote by Frantz Fanon is the primary reason many readers of this book may refuse to revalidate their indoctrinated religious belief. Many don't even realize that whatever they belief is as a result of years of indoctrination and not by free will. The human mind through its magnetic character can turn a blatant lie to truth and make it work as the truth through the metaphysical energy of the human mind. Whatever religious believe we hold today is a product of the environment we were born into. Only few people are able to overcome the force of indoctrination and put on the garment of reasoning and reality.

The fact that there are many views of God points to the fact that mankind is still in search of a God, some abandoning their God in search of a more renowned God, given power to this God and even acting on his behalf. Is God truly JAHWEH, JESUS CHRIST,

ALLAH, BUDHA, JEHOVAH, etc.? Does God actually exist? No, they are not God. The only universal deity is NATURE and nature actually exists.

The last definition given by wikionart.org is the real definition of God, "God is the (personification of the) laws of nature".

Nature is the embodiment of everything in the universe and the laws that govern them.

Let the truth reveal itself, stop religious indoctrination of children; parent all over the world should keep their children off religious gathering. They will grow, without influence of organize religion, to discover their individual Gods through original genetic adaptation, modification and experience, the ancient of our forbearer. What you discover through reasoning, research and unadulterated consciousness is the truth, that's your God and you will be surprised because they will discover nature, the only true 'God'.

The study of nature which is science is the only true religion and the application of nature which is technology is the only true miracle. Scientifics laws, dogma and doctrine are universal signifying truth.

Countries that are verse in science are more develop than countries that are verse in religion signifying the presence of God.

Science studies the true God while religions study an imaginary God. Say no to mental slavery, free yourself from the shackles of religion. Mental slavery is the worst form of slavery, it gives you the illusion of freedom, makes you trust, love and defend your oppressor and their institution while making enemy of those who are trying to free you or open your eye.

The presence of different religions with different dogma and doctrines is evidence of a misconception somewhere.

The spread and acceptance of other people's God while relegating your indigenous God, instead of evolving him through adaptation, research and modification is evidence of man's success in dominating another not evidence of truth because it is not universal. It cannot be proven beyond reasonable doubt and it was spread by violence and suppression. Christianity spread to Africa by the Europeans whose sole aim was to subdue the people. They came with two gifts; the Bible and the gun. Christianity was never accepted by free will neither was Islam.

We can invariable say God manifested himself in nature. He did not create nature, he is nature. Study him and unlock the secrets of the universe. God is gravity, uranium, gold, air, sand, crude oil, trees, law of conservation of energy, laws of motions, laws of thermodynamic, laws of aerodynamic etc., use them and fulfill your destiny, oh black Africa.

The evil of Christianity as a tool for enslavement was revealed in this letter.

Letter[15] from one of the most evil King Leopold II of Belgium to Colonial Missionaries, 1883
(This speech reveals the motives and methods of colonialism. It shows that the relations between the former colonialists and the formerly subjected peoples have not changed in substance but in its sophistication.)
....Reverend Fathers and Dear Compatriots; the task asked of you to

accomplish is very delicate and demands much tact and diplomacy. Fathers, you are going to preach the Gospel, but your preaching must be inspired by first, the interest of the Belgium government state. The main goal of your mission in the Congo is not to teach the Negro the knowledge of God, because they already know him. They talk and commit themselves to their God. They know that killing, stealing, adultery and blasphemy are not good. Your role essentially will be to easily facilitate the task of the administrative and industrial personnel. That is to say, you will interpret the gospel in a way to protect and serve the interest of Belgium, in that part of the world. To do so you will see that our savages be not interested in the riches that their soil possesses in order that they not want them. Thus, they be not involved in murderous competition with us and dream to live a luxurious life.

Your knowledge of the scriptures will help us to use special text that recommended the fidels to love poverty such as, "The Beatitudes", "Blessed are the poor, for theirs is the Kingdom"; "It is hard for the rich to enter the Kingdom of Heaven". You will do all that you can to cause the Negro to fear being rich in order that they may go to heaven. From time to time, keep them from rebelling and to keep them in fear that you will use violence. You will teach them to endure anything, even when they are insulted or beaten by your compatriots (administrative). You will teach them that whosoever uses vengeance is not a child of God. You will cause them to follow the example of the Saints who turned the other cheek. You will take them away from anything or act that procures them with the courage to confront us. I am alluding myself here to their magic, i.e., Ju-Ju, Voodoo. They should not feel like abandoning their Ju-Ju, and you will do your best to take them away at the same time. Your action will be essentially on the younger people that might not rebel. If the commandment of the Father is contradictory to the parents, the child should learn to obey what the missionary teaches him because he is the father of his soul. We must force them into submission and obedience.

Dear compatriots, these are some of the principles you must apply, you will find many more in the book that will be given to you at the end of this session. Teach the Gospel to the Negroes in an African style, in order that they are kept submissive to the White colonist.

They would not rebel against the injustice done to them by the colonist. Make them always meditate on "Blessed be those that weep/cry; for theirs is the Kingdom of Heaven." Convert the Blacks always by means of the whip. Keep their wives in submission for nine months, so they can work for you graciously. Require from them an offering of recognition to you; goats, chickens, eggs, each time you visit their village.

Avoid, by all means, the Blacks becoming rich. Cause them to each and every day that it's "Impossible for a rich man to enter Heaven". Make them pay tithes each Sunday for church. Utilize this money, that is intended for the poor, for our own business investments. Institute a system of confession which will make you good detectives in order to denounce/put down every Black which has a spirit of rebellion against the system. Teach the Negroes that their

statues, idols, are works of the devil, confiscate them and fill our museums with them. Teach the Negro to forget about their heroes in order to worship and give praise to ours. Don't give a seat to a Negro when they come to see you, at the most just give him a cigarette.
Don't invite him to break bread with you, even if he gave you a chicken every time you went to see him. Consider all blacks as little children, and require from them to refer to you as father. My dear compatriots; if you apply to the letter all this, the interest of Belgium in the Congo will be protected for many centuries. I thank you.
King Leopold II
(Translated from French by Prince Asiel Center for International Studies, USA)
"The above speech which shows the real intention of the Christian missionary journey in Africa was exposed to the world by Mr. Moukouani Muikwani Bukoko, born in the Congo in 1915, and who in 1935 while working in the Congo, bought a second hand Bible from a Belgian priest who forgot the speech in the Bible. -- Dr. Chiedozie Okoro"

CHAPTER FIVE

HOW TO ACCESS GOD

THE UNIVERSALITY OF GOD

In this mysterious universe, there is one thing which a man can feel certain of, that thing is nature and it accompanied laws. Man has come to harness radio waves for wireless communication which is evident in radio, television and mobile phones, man has converted the sun ray to electrical and mechanical energy, man set a chain reaction from an element of nature; uranium, man has been able to carry out kidney transplant, produces machines to speed up work. Men has shown that the power of God dwell in them. These are true miracles, the continuation of creation and evolution.

Man himself is certainly one of the presence in the universe; he is part of nature, part of God. Therefore, man's greatest goal is to seek for other presence in the universe with the aim of harnessing and utilizing these presences. Such search is the true search of God.

For centuries, mankind has searched, with greater or lesser zeal, to find those absolute realities and he has altered, capitalized on, discovered, explained and made use of this reality. That reality is nature, her resources and laws. The study of nature God called science is the ultimate search for God.

The greatest of all is nature and her accompanied and operational laws. In this the secret of the world is embedded, in this creation and evolution continues. A careful study of this is the true study of God. Think of the ability to transmit wireless message across the Atlantic Ocean, is there a greater miracle than that? Think of the ability to transmit electron in a wire, hence producing electricity, think of the ability to produce artificial leg for the amputee or healing to the sick using natural element and herbs. There is no greater miracle than that which already exists in nature. True miracle is effective use of nature otherwise called technology.

The best thing is that these nature and her laws are universal, therefore God is universal because God is nature and he is accessible to all. God did not create nature, rather he manifested himself as nature, and he is nature not a person with gender and name.

Each major religion has evolved to explain the unexplained part of nature and her manifestation, given that reality a different name, depending on what your religion may be but Christians gives that reality name, gender and personality- God- the Supreme Being.

God in many ways and in different times have proven himself to be whatever natural thing you call him. Those days in Africa, people worship God by any means possible; some worship him by means of the sun, the moon, stars, trees and graving images. Some by means of assembling some woods together, some erecting a structure of human semblance, some tying white and red clothes to a tree and spraying blood of fowls and other small animals to it and making incantations- that is their prayer. Many names were attributed to him- Chi-ukwu, Abasi, Obong, Oduduwa, Egbesu, etc in those days.

In this recent time, the tables are turned. The coming of the Christian God brought an end to the old ways of search; making the old ways outdated and barbaric. Many dropped the old way and go for an imaginary God, the God of the tribes of Israel.

To access the true God, we must study and harness the laws of nature for in it is everything we ever desire or wish for in life. In it there is financial breakthrough, good financial education, discovery and invention. In it there is Divine protection through the law of karma and weaponry technology. In it there is miracle of the womb through artificial fertility and insemination. In nature there is treatment for every kind of ailment and diseases, in nature there is elimination of poverty through application of sound economic laws and good financial education. In nature there is power to build and destroyed the world. God can be harnessed and accessed by everyone because God is nature. You don't need an arbitrator called pastor.

With all the falsehood, deceit, manipulation and cheating, the best option is for everyone to device a mean to access God, to communicate with God and received blessing without the aid or assistance of the so called men of God.

Why the 10,000, 50,000 or 100,000 seat auditorium? The best way to avoid the snare of fake men of God is to learn how to seek your God directly. Be a man of God for yourself.

Matthew 6:6

> "But you, when you pray, go into your room, and when you have
> shut your door, pray to your Father who is in secret place,
> and your Father who sees in secret will reward you openly"

"In secret..."-you don't need your church The biblical God says that you are a priest. Peter is saying that the two benefits that priests have are now available to everyone who is a believer;

In the Old Testament, priests did two things:

1. They had the right, privilege, and responsibility to go

directly to God. They could pray and talk to God, worship, and fellowship with God. Everybody else had to go through a priest.

2. The priest had the privilege and responsibility of representing God to the people and ministering to the needs of other people (serving).

Those are the two important things when you become a believer.

You now have direct access to God. You don't have to pray through a priest or anybody else. You don't have to confess through anybody else. You don't have to fellowship with God through anybody else or through any organized religion. Talk with the Lord and fellowship directly with him.

The Bible says that when Jesus died on the cross, there was a veil in the temple that separated the Holy of Holies, where God's Spirit was, from where man was. Only priests could go behind that veil once a year. When Jesus died on the cross, God ripped that veil –about 70 feet –from top to bottom, symbolizing that there is no longer a barrier, signifying that everyone now have direct access to God. Matthew 27;50-51

Why are you still confused even when your bible has stated the obvious? Why do you worship the God of your pastor as if he is different from other Christian God?

It is not late, you can always return to him and he will heal you.

Hosea 6:1-2

"Come, and let us return to the LORD; for He has torn, but He will heal us; He has stricken, but He will bind us up"

> *After two days He will revive us; on the third day*
> *He will raise us up, that we may live in His sight".*

Acts 17:27

> *"So that they should seek the Lord, in the hope that*
> *they might grope for Him and find Him, though*
> *He is not far from each one of us"*

God is not in Israel or mecca, God is nature and nature is universal. God is in Africa, He is on the sand you match, the air you breathe, the plant you eat, the water you drink and in you.

To access God, you must free your mind from all forms of indoctrinated belief, emancipate yourself from mental slavery. Believe that nothing about religion is the truth, clear your mind and start a fresh search for the truth without subjecting yourself to one dogma or doctrine. At the end, a self-revealing truth will surface.

Be a Christian, Muslim, Buddhist and Jew at the same time.

STATE OF YOUR MIND

> *"Blessed are the pure in heart, for they shall see God" Matthew 5:8*

What is purity? It simply means free from all external factors, free from pollution and contamination. Blessed are those whose heart is free from religious, cultural, political and economic pollution and contamination for they shall see God, that's exactly what the bible says.

Each element or substance in the universe has her original constituent, what they are made up of originally. Whenever anything is added to it, it becomes polluted. For instance, water is made up of hydrogen and oxygen, any substance added to water pollutes it from its purest form.

When a child is born, his heart is pure without any form of thought. Return to your childhood.

Before western civilization, there was African civilization, before western and Arabic religion, there was African religion. This was the original Africa. Anything copied today are pollution, for you to see God, you must free yourself from this pollution.

The bible in essence is saying that if you free your mind from all form of indoctrination, you shall see God.

The mind is the center of all thoughts both good and bad. The mind is the force of attraction, the conscious engine that attracts the unconscious. The mind is the center of human energy. The mind is the tool for accessing God; it is your personal pastor.

Even in our contemporary life, the state of your mind has the efficacy to affect all other parts of the body in all its ramifications and has the power either to destroy or build you forever. The state of our emotion affects our judgment at a particular time.

Science has discovered many laws in the universe, from gravity, aerodynamic, conservation of energy, relativity and the newton's laws of motions. There are many yet hidden, some are social laws, some are psychological. We will explain one of these laws.

Magnetic character of the human mind

This law states that whatever your mind conceive, believe and work for its actualization under motivation, the force of nature(part of God) will bring the resources, the circumstance of life, the knowledge and the people needed to actualize this goal as you work towards it in a definite direction, the only hindrance is time.

Our mind has the power to attract the forces, circumstances of life and resources that are in consonance to our dominant thought. That's why people with poverty mentality will continue to be poor despite all the prayers and fasting they offer to Nature God.

This is why a mentally poor man will remain poor even when a large sum of money is given to him.

Most people are unaware of the metaphysical realization of the mind's energy when it is concentrated, which causes miracle/magic to be experienced according to the degree of concentration, believe and motivation.

In the Sermon on the Mount —the beatitudes, Christ stated the criterion for the kingdom of God, howbeit; the easiest way to access God- a pure heart. How pure is your heart?

Nature and tradition permitted it, the laws governing the universe concedes with it that whatever a man sows, that he will certainly reap.

Human being is made up of matter and energy, the center of human energy is the mind. The mind can be stimulated mostly externally but sometime internally to produce "miracle". A stimulated mind can cure HIV/AIDS by releasing hormone to the body; a stimulated mind can cure itself of any sickness.

The process in which religious leaders used to do supposedly "miracle" is by mind stimulation which works through the magnetic character of the human mind. This follower went to church with a total conviction and believed in the ability of their pastor to heal them, this conviction generate an energy which act in consonance with their dominant desire, to attract the forces, circumstance, resources and all other things necessary to actualize this dominant thought, hence its manifestation called miracle. This thing can act with total conviction and believe in tree, stone, water and anything.

However, this attractive power of the mind does require practical work, consistency and true knowledge in the field of your dominant thought. It does not only require faith, belief, prayer and fasting to attract your dominant thought to reality but it requires practical work and scientific process. Generally, the motive will drive you above any obstacle and failure you may encounter while working toward this dominant goal.

Jeremiah 6:16

"Thus says the LORD: stand in the ways and see, and ask for

the old paths, where the good way is, and walk in it; then you will

find rest for your souls. But they said, 'we will not walk in it"

To access God, you must clean your heart from all sorts of evil, indoctrination, envy and embrace science and reality as they are a barrier between you and nature.

James 4:8. "

Draw near to God and He will draw near to you. Cleanse your hands, you sinners; and purify your hearts, you double-minded"

I watched a movie depicting the story of a lady who was betrothed to a palm wine tapper but later betrothed to a rich farmer by her parent who happened to spot her during a new yam festival. The palm wine tapper got angry, went to a river, sworn that the woman will never see peace and drown himself, sealing the spoken word with his blood.

Her four children die before the age of four; she cried in each occasion and moved on. She was accused of witchcraft and of eating her children. Her husband got married to another woman and abandoned her to her ordeal. Finally she gave birth to a set of twins after a prolonged period of barrenness; male and female.

At the age of four, the male twin developed similar symptoms as of his late siblings and died within days. Soon the daughter developed similar symptoms and the woman, engulfed with grief, bitterness, anger, she resolve that this one will not die!

She visited herbalist and they told her nothing can be done. She met a woman who narrated to her how she lost her family during the Nigerian civil war and decided to take her to an herbalist (native doctor).

On their way to the herbalist, they saw an old man standing on the side of the road, they went pass him. The herbalist equally informs them that nothing can be done, they left.

On their way back, they saw this same man standing on the exact spot they saw him previously. The man beckons to her, why did you want to bury a life child. She was astonished, the man said he can help her and that her friend should go. She had little option and was willing to do anything to ensure her daughter is alive.

The man took her to a mountain; told her to wait while he proceeds to the top of the mountain. After some moment, he came back to ask her whether she is ready to give her life in exchange for her child, she agreed.

After the necessary rituals, the man told her that she is rejected; all what is needed is the child. Due to her resilient, the man was more willing to help her, he narrated the source of her ordeal and warned her never to relate anything she hears or see to anyone for the day she does, she will die.

He took the child further up the mountain and stayed all night. When morning beckons, he did not return. After the mother waited for some hours to no avail, she went up the mountain, lo and behold, the man laid dead, the surrounding was distorted as if some serious fighting occurred. The child, she laid there, alive. She took her child and went home.

At the age of 25, a born again Christian, the girl travelled home during new yam festival and narrated to her mother who never went to church that she saw her mother being lifted up in celestial honor with angels singing praises to her in her dream.

It was then the mother narrated the entire story to her. She told her daughter that was the day she met her God. She died few days later. That was God and she accessed him because she was resolved never to let her child die. Have you resolved to meet God, to solve your problem and ready to follow all your good ideas to fruition?

You may call it movie but according to the producer, it is based on true life story.

When you set your mind to achieved anything and there is a price to pay if you fail, nature permit the attraction of the resources, people, circumstance of life and knowledge needed to actualize this thing closer to you. However, you need to make practical moves.

This is the principle of accessing God. The idea of praying, singing, fasting, attending churches and mosque are all absurd. God is not present in any of these places. Study the life of super-rich men and you will understand the power of the mind, the warehouse to harness nature.

Jeremiah 29:13.

> *"And you will seek Me and find Me, when you search for Me with all your heart"*

Stop following dogma, ask question.

How open is your heart? Can you find a place to doubt your present pastor, be pure without belief, and move by the spirit of search and scrutiny alone?

Matthew 5:8.

> *"Blessed are the pure in heart, for they shall see God"*

Move to a quiet place, place your taught on what you want to do and the consequence if you fail. Meditate and pour out your heart, start creating strategies and how-to, write them down. When it stops flowing, start implementing your ideas. More ideas will be created during the course of implementation, this is how nature works. If you are persistent, and have something to lose if you fail, the forces of nature will set you on the path of success. The present noisy churches are not the best place to beseech God.

The state of your mind gives you access to God, to wealth, healing and whatever you can think of. God present himself in so many manners and depending on your need. God is not a person, he does not have a choosing people, he does not belong to any religion, God is universal, and God is nature.

A contact to the best doctor when you are sick is God while a pastor who insisted on prayers only is Devil.

A village herbalist advising you on your heritage history and offers a practical remedy is God while a pastor insisting on fasting and prayer is devil.

A friend offering assistance in time of need is God while a relative who claim to love you but refuse to assist is Devil.

A teacher who instructs you that success comes from planning and execution is God while the one who said success comes from believing in God, paying your tithe, praying and fasting is Devil.

There is never a rigid rule to obtain blessing or commune with God, circumstance determine the rule but your state of mind is the pre-requisite. A mentally enslave mind can never access God.

How exactly can you acquire this state of mind that gives you communion with God?

Understand that God is nature and can be accessed by everyone

Believe that you have the right to communicate with God directly in anyplace and at any time, not through anyone. It is not a right for few privileged people but for all.

Study, experiment, practice and adopt nature and its accompanied laws. Believe that you can, achieve, overcome or accomplish whatever you desire.

Think of the implication of failure not in the context of fear of failure, but in the context of what to loose or suffer if you fail. Be determined to succeed, be moved by a strong motive.

Then, seek God through planning, execution, evaluation, education, research, experimentation, practice and learning. You will always need practical and physical knowledge to succeed not just prayer and holistic faith. You will always need true knowledge of nature to heal yourself of any sickness.

Then finally, get up and move toward your desire using practical and visible plan.

BY FAITH
Hebrews 11:6.
> *"But without faith it is impossible to please Him, for he who comes to God must believe that He is, and that He is a rewarder of those who diligently seek Him".*

God is nature and nature rewards those who seek and play to its rules. Nature is vast that's why majority do not seek him, he holds the answer to virtually everything in life, and the study of nature is called science.

Science made nation to conquer other nations, Europe was able to conquered Africa because of their shipping and navigation technology. The most powerful nations in the world are good in science and technology. This is the reward for all those who diligently seek God.

Religion today is sustained by fear not by faith. Majority cannot separate faith from fear; the fear of God, fear of hell, fear of discrimination if ever declare the absurdity of religion, fear of devil; an imaginary being created by our mind power, fear of people. History proves that religion is built by fear and terror.

Faith is application of true knowledge in pursuit of life goals and desire, with an insurmountable believe that you will succeed.

You don't just have faith, you deliberately acquire faith. True knowledge is truth that can be proven beyond reasonable doubt to be real, correct, effective, realistic etc.

The definition of faith in the bible as the substance of things hoped for, the evidence of things not seen is wrong. Hebrew 11:1

Nature makes it possible for knowledge to breed belief, and belief to manifest faith, and faith with mentally revolution mind set manifest in the physical, whatsoever you desire. Place your faith in yourself, your drive, desire and motive, and you shall be a man of God. Propagate true freedom and you shall be a man of God. Place your faith on science and technology and you shall become a superior people, the choosing people of God. Have true faith and you shall access God.

Humans are made up of matter and energy, the mind is the Centre of the energy. Focus it, liberate yourself from mental slavery, and propagate the ideology of self-reliance; a true political, economic, technological, cultural and religious independence. Through this, you will commune with nature God in reality and according to your dictate.

"God will bless someone today" is a baseless statement.

"Tell your neighbor that your problem is over" is an odd statement.

Look around the world; do you think it is a place that you can live without problem? Be reasonable and you will understand the meaning of mental slavery because that is the only reason you belief and thundered "Amen" to such absurd and unrealistic statements.

Maybe the misconception is from the definition of problems, what are the areas in our life we experience what we call problems; they are finance, health, family, insecurity, choice of spouse and inter/external relationship.

Why do you believe you need a divine help to be financially buoyant when money is physically printed. A good financial education could do the job perfectly, in your own accord. Money is simply an instrument for measuring wealth. Wealth is a product of productive mental attitude of a person or collective productive mental attitude of the people.

Faith forms the embodiment of all things- visible and invisible; seen and the unseen. It is the greatest virtue given to humanity. In it lies the power to succeed even when all fails, but then, a liberated mind is the key and practical attempts are necessary. Scientific discovery and technology are not done purely by faith but by research, test, try and error. This is how God is accessed.

In the Bible, faith is the substance of things hoped for, the evidence of things not seen. Workable faith does not end here.

Believe emancipate faith. What you believe shape your faith and your reality. If you do not adopt a scientific study process in your conclusion, you may be doom. If your believe system is based on years of indoctrination and societal influence, you do not by will believe in what you believed.

Believing by will comes from informed and liberated mind, I believed in self-reliance. This is the foundation of the faith used in accessing God; in accessing science and technology; in accessing a united Africa, a union state of Africa; in accessing a common African gold currency; in accessing African legion.

Abraham is a perfect example, in the Christian realm; he is called the father of faith. He never performed any showman, he never spoke in an unknown tongue, he never worked any form of miracle yet he was a friend of God. The Christians of this day regard him as an epitome of faith. His faith made him a righteous man; many times in the bible, about three times in the bible he is called God's friend- his faith defined him as God's friend and the father of faith. - Isaiah 41:8, 2 Chronicles 20:7, James 2:23, Faith is an absolute confidence on the things not seen. A total conviction of something not here; faith unites all things and from it emanates loyalty, devotion, self-reliance, trust, confidence and hope. Always bear in mind that faith without work is void, meaning faith without knowledge is void.

Thus Abraham in the bible showed a strong faith. He left his home with his wife and followed the voice of God irrespective of all his ordeals. Even when there seem no possibilities of success, his faith gets stronger. Faith is the principal virtue and the basis for accessing God. It gives you ground.

Moses is another example; he became a wanderer when he ran out of Egypt. To him, he is running away from the king who has ordered him death, to him, he is running away from the Egyptian army who are busy seeking his life, he is running away from the calumnies of the people. He became a wanderer.

In his bid to survive all the odds around him and to satisfy the father in law, he met face to face with the almighty-the true God, the manifestation of nature. He believed God and followed his instructions; he fought the greatest battle in Egypt, leading the people of Israelites to an unknown land, even when there seem no possibilities of surviving. He was called a man of God in the Bible.

It was through practical faith based on true knowledge that Marconi carried out the first experiment to transmit wireless message across the Atlantic ocean, it was through practical faith based on true knowledge that Ojukwu of eastern Nigeria attempted to succeed from Nigeria, it was through faith that the wright brothers flew the first air plane, it was through practical faith that Thomas Edison built the light bulb, it was through faith that

INNOSON produced the first made in Nigeria cars and trucks, it was through faith that Dr Abalaka claimed and challenged that he has found the treatment for AIDS.

Most people misconstrued faith to be religious, faith is psychological in nature. It works with the human mind in accordance with the magnetic character of the mind irrespective of religion, creed, believe, dogma or tribe. Faith is natural.

In conclusion, the best man of God is you. Wake up from your slumber, stop being deceived by the acclaimed men of God, pick up the mantle and become a man of God for yourself and for the glory of Africa.

BIBLIOGRAPHY

1. https://www.marxists.org/subject/africa/lumumba/1960/06/independence.htm
   Source: Patrice Lumumba, The Truth about a Monstrous Crime of the Colonialists, Moscow, Foreign Languages Publishing House, 1961, pp. 44-47.

2. Martin Meredith(2011) The State of Africa: the history of the continent since independence. 2nd edi. Pp 99

3. www.brainyquote.com/quotes/m/marcus_garvey.html

4. www.nationalhumanitiesscenter.org/tserve/twenty/tkeyinfo/garvey.htm

5. http://panafricannews.blogspot.com/2012/09/kwame-nkrumah-speech-at-founding.html

6. http://www.thomassankara.net/spip.php?article769&lang=fr

7. Thomas Sankara speaks(1988) by Pathfinder Press
   Source: http://www.gngwane.com/2010/10/thomas-sankara-in-his-own-words.html

8. http://biography.yourdictionary.com/chukwuemeka-odumegwu-ojukwu

9. www.blackpast.org/biafras-declaration-independence-1967

10   http://www.infoplease.com/ipa/A0001462.html#ixzz3CwYoLVFK

11   http://www.infoplease.com/ipa/A0001463.html#ixzz3CwYMdmVV

12   http://www.infoplease.com/ipa/A0001468.html

13   http://www.infoplease.com/ipa/A0001470.html#ixzz3CwUKJF00

14   Godhttp://hughwilliamson.hubpages.com/hub/10-Brilliant-Scientists-and-Their-View-of-God

15   http://www.afrikaglobalnetwork.com/htm/leopold.htm

www.ingramcontent.com/pod-product-compliance
Lightning Source LLC
Chambersburg PA
CBHW031352040426
42444CB00005B/262